Making Greetings Cards
for Beginners

Making
Greetings Cards
for Beginners

Pat Sutherland

GUILD OF MASTER CRAFTSMAN PUBLICATIONS

First published 1998 by
Guild of Master Craftsman Publications Ltd,
166 High Street, Lewes, East Sussex, BN7 1XU

© Pat Sutherland 1998

Cover photograph and photographs of finished cards by Dennis Bunn
All other photographs by Ken Amer

ISBN 1 86108 047 6

Designed by Teresa Dearlove

Set in Novarese

Printed and bound by Kyodo Printing (Singapore)
under the supervision of MRM Graphics, Winslow, Bucks., UK

Acknowledgements

A special thank you to Ken Amer for the excellent photographs of work in progress which appear throughout the book. Many thanks to Hazel Shearer, and to Mr Sonke of The Heritage Rubber Company, 92 Grove Street, Edinburgh for all their help in supplying, and advice on using, rubber stamps and embossing powder. Thanks to Neil Stevenson and his staff of Business Equipment Services, Kirkwall, Orkney, for making copies for me. Many thanks to Betty Laughton for the beautiful knitwear I have used in this book, and for her support.

Contents

To Bruce,
Craig and Ian Sutherland,
with love

Introduction

Greetings cards have been sent and received for a very long time. The first valentines were sent in the eighteenth century, when they would have been made by the sender and contained home-produced drawings and verses. By the nineteenth century, shops were selling valentines which, although still handmade, were being produced commercially. At this time cards became increasingly elaborate, adorned with feathers, lace or even real flowers. The mid-nineteenth century also saw the advent of commercially produced, handmade Christmas cards.

By the mid-twentieth century the elaborate, work-intensive greetings cards had given way to mass-produced, printed cards of all kinds and handmade cards ceased to be valued. Recently, however, there has been a rise in appreciation of handcrafted goods and individual card craftsmen are again finding a market for their wares.

The only drawback in this upsurge of handmade cards is the price. A man is worthy of his hire, and the time and effort expended on a complicated card has to be reflected in its selling price, which is often high. One of the reasons for this book is to allow people to send well-made, handcrafted cards without breaking the bank.

The other reason for this book is to combat the widely held belief that it is necessary to buy expensive craft items because the general mass of people are unable to produce such cards themselves. There is no mystique to creating attractive handmade cards. Care is all that is required, and a card produced with love and care is bound to be appreciated by its recipient. How many people are depriving themselves of the pleasure to be gained from creating their own cards – not knowing what they are missing?

The cards in this book are not complicated. By following the instructions for each project you can soon be producing cards that give you, and your friends and family, great pleasure.

As well as Christmas, birthday, valentine and humorous cards, etc., I have intentionally designed quite a few cards for no specific purpose so that they can be used for any occasion with the addition of an appropriate message, or as a letter card or notelet. Please add any words to the fronts of any of the cards if that suits your needs better. Once you have mastered the basics you will be able to adapt and improve the cards in any way that you like.

I have included a lengthy chapter on Materials and Techniques which covers more than you will strictly need to know to be able to make any of the card projects. Please take time to read it, and take note that you may use whatever you have to hand in most cases. This is a beginners' book and you may not wish to make more than a few cards. My aim is to show you that you do not need to rush out to your local art shop and buy large amounts of expensive equipment and paints, which may never be used again, for any of these projects. If you find a particular type of card which you do wish to make again, and from experience feel that different materials and tools might produce a better product or speed things up, then you can investigate what is available. Where I consider that the best result can only be achieved by a specific material, I have named it; elsewhere, do feel free to use what you have.

You may be surprised by some of the items used in the projects – the photo-

copier, for instance. We may be looking back to a past time when craftsmen created cards and mass production was still far in the future, but there is no need for us to ignore modern innovations which can help us. Photocopying is a marvellous way to copy, enlarge or reduce any picture and is so much simpler than the methods used in the past that its use should be encouraged wherever practicable.

In every high street there is either a copy shop dedicated to supplying photocopies to the general public or a stationer's where the staff will happily make copies for you and will be full of advice on how best to proceed. This is where I go myself. If, like me, you come to make quite a lot of cards with the assistance of the photocopier, your local shop staff will get to know you and will be happy to solve problems for you as they occur. As you will discover, some machines have an unfortunate habit of leaving an unprinted strip down the edge of copies; if your local shop cannot find a way around this they may be willing to trim off the offending area at no extra charge.

Another place which will undertake photocopying for you is your local library, but in my experience the charges they make are rather higher than the other two options. A fourth alternative is the self-service machines which are now becoming common in newsagents' shops.

Although some of the projects in this book advocate the use of a copier, in most cases alternative ways of proceeding are suggested. However, if possible, do try using the copier – you will be impressed with the results.

The word processor is another modern machine which I think you should consider using to help you. In the Variations section of the 'Happy Birthday' project (no. 9) I have suggested that if you are unhappy with your handwriting you could try creating the duplicated greeting with a word processor or computer. These machines are now in many private homes and workplaces and can provide a wonderful variety of different sizes and styles of font. If you do not have access to one, however, do not worry – this is entirely optional.

Something which might concern some readers is the use throughout this book of metric measurement. Many people, I know, still think in feet and inches. I have given all measurements in centimetres, but do not be alarmed – simply arm yourself with a ruler which has centimetres on it and resist the temptation to try to compare the measurements with imperial. Where it says 'add a centimetre', use the ruler to measure and add a centimetre. What could be simpler?

Finally, I do hope that you enjoy making these cards and that you will be pleased with the response you get from your friends and family. If you are inspired to go further, try some of the variations I suggest or make any that have occurred to you as you have been working. The final chapter will give you some ideas on what you might do with your cards once you have made them. As in most hobbies the finished article can start to crowd you out of house and home unless you find some sort of an outlet for it.

Materials and Techniques

Before beginning to make any of the projects in this book, be sure to collect together all the materials you will need; these are listed at the beginning of each project. This chapter introduces all the materials and methods which we will be using, apart from a few which are self-explanatory.

In keeping with my policy of using what you already have, I suggest that you use this guide to glues as a reference. In the card projects where I feel only one glue is suitable, I have specified that glue clearly; otherwise you should use what you have or are happy to use.

Pritt Stick

Many households already have this useful push-up glue stick. It works like a lipstick and is rubbed over the area to be glued. Because it is a 'dry' adhesive, leaving a sticky film but no moisture, it is very clean to use and does not cause delicate papers and fabrics to buckle and distort. It is odour-free and non-toxic. I have used this a great deal in this book, but this does not always mean that no other glue would do.

Copydex

This is a rubber adhesive which comes in a jar with a brush in the

Adhesives

lid, or in a tube. It is white but dries almost clear. It can be a 'dry' adhesive if painted on and left until tacky before putting the item to be glued onto it. Laid on thick and wet, it will glue quite rough materials. On some surfaces any excess glue can be rubbed off with a finger once dry. It will come away like stringy rubber. Do test the surface before attempting this. Ideally, it is better to glue sparingly than to try to remove excess.

Copydex is almost odour-free and non-toxic. However, it should be kept off clothes, as once dry it is not easy to remove.

Spray Adhesive

This adhesive, which also comes as a low-tack repositionable type, applies a fine, even layer of glue to any surface. Any object to be glued should be put on a surface covered in newspapers, as the glue tends to spread over a wide area. If you intend to use it a lot you could make a spraying box by removing one side of a large cardboard box so that the item to be sprayed can lie inside and the excess glue will be contained by the sides. One draw back of spray adhesive is that it is quite expensive compared to other methods.

CAUTION Use in a well-ventilated room, or outside, as it is solvent-based and strong-smelling.

Double-Sided Tape

This clever tape comes with a waxed-paper backing on one side and a sticky surface on the other. Once it is stuck in place the waxed paper is removed, exposing the sticky back on which to stick your object. It can be fiddly to remove the backing from double-sided tape but it is a useful, clean alternative to glues in many projects.

PVA Glue

This is a strong glue which will stick most materials. Although opaque white when in use, it dries clear. It is very versatile and can be used neat or diluted. When very dilute it will also stiffen paper or fabric and work as a varnish. PVA is fast-drying, which is very useful when working on projects where each stage has to dry before you proceed. However, it can only be removed from clothes etc. while still wet. Used extensively in schools, PVA is non-toxic and odourless.

If you have any difficulty finding it, PVA can be found in DIY shops as wood glue – but read the labels, as there are many kinds of wood glue.

Card and Paper

Card

Every project in this book, except the two which use bought window cards, is based on a sheet of photocopier card in the standard A4 size. This is readily available from stationers and comes in a good variety of colours. This material has been chosen as it is easy to find, is already cut to the right size, and fits standard C5-size envelopes when folded as a card. It is very inexpensive.

Heavier card may be used for some projects if preferred, but cannot be used on the photocopier.

Water-Colour Paper

Moderately thick water-colour paper in A4 pads will give you a good substitute for A4 card if by any chance you cannot get it. It comes in a variety of surfaces. Some types of paper are more textured than others and are not able to be put through a photocopier as some projects demand – choose a smooth variety for this. For both the 'Simple Landscape' and the 'Abstract Landscape' projects (nos. 13 and 15) I have used a smooth cartridge paper in different-sized pads, which are sold for painting or drawing on. The surface will withstand the scrubbing of paint across it

in the latter project, yet is pliable enough to be easy to glue for the former.

Copy Paper

Copy paper is the A4 white paper used in typewriters or computer printers. It is freely available, good-quality and cheap. In some situations, with a clear image, it can be used as tracing paper, as is the case in some of these projects. I have sometimes used photocopier paper where white scrap paper is called for.

Bought Window Cards

Window cards can be bought from craft shops and are made in three sections which fold together over an insert. It is worth taking some time to see how they fit together before you actually use one in a project. Section A folds over and is stuck to section B, enclosing your chosen insert.

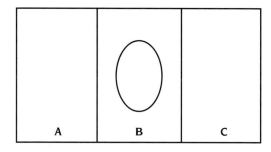

Bought window card. A is stuck to B to contain insert

Brown Paper

Brown paper is used in one project and can be easily found as wrapping paper or paper bags. Choose a good strong paper that will not buckle when wet with glue, or use a 'dry' glue (see Adhesives) with thinner brown papers.

Tissue Paper

Tissue paper is lightweight and semi-opaque; it is not strong, wet or dry. Colours may run, so try not to brush over too often with glue, and dispose of damp pieces carefully to protect your clothes and furniture. Tissue paper can be bought in packs from art shops, and although you will have to buy more than you need for one project, it can always be used for gift wrapping or to protect precious things.

Newspaper

Newspaper is quite adequate for many situations where you need scrap paper to mask, or protect, parts of a project or for trying out pens, stamps etc. Where there is a danger of the print rubbing off onto the work, plain white scrap paper will be specified.

Copying Methods

Carbon Paper

Most people are familiar with carbon paper, which makes an exact copy on the paper under it when pressed on from above. If you do not mind damaging the original, you can lay first the carbon paper and then your picture onto your card, and by tracing the outline of the picture transfer it to the card. This would be possible in the 'Photocopy and Wash' project (no. 14) if you were trying to do something similar without a photocopier.

Tracing

You can buy tracing paper in pads from art shops. However, for tracing pictures I prefer to use clear plastic – either plastic file sleeves or the plastic sheet sold by stationers for use with overhead projectors. These are both perfectly clear and it is easy to see the picture you are tracing through them. Most other firm, clear plastic (such as plastic bags) would do a similar job, but is fragile. The plastic sheets are particularly firm and long-lasting if you want to keep them to use more than once. Just make sure that you are using a permanent felt-tipped pen with a fine point so that the ink adheres. Some pens smudge, so cover the part you have already done with white paper or newsprint rather than let your arm rub over it.

Photocopier

See Introduction.

Cutting Tools

Craft Knives/Circular Cutter and Self-Healing Mat

Craft knives and scalpels are freely available and inexpensive but should be kept fitted with a sharp, fresh blade or they will tear card. Craft knives are especially good for cutting around curves and awkward shapes, but as they are very sharp you should always cut away from your other hand so as to avoid accidents.

If you have one of the circular cutters which are sold in craft shops for cutting out patchwork pieces, you may prefer to use this instead. The cutting wheel is safer than a craft knife, and the accompanying mat, which 'heals' itself, can help to avoid slips, and so is good to use with a knife too. The cutting wheel cannot be used for internal cuts like windows, and unfortunately is, together with its mat, very expensive.

Cutting Board and Ruler

A large cutting board and a metal ruler are essential accessories when using a craft knife. These do not have to be bought specially. The cutting board could be a large breadboard or even an old, thick telephone book.

Pinking Shears

These are strong scissors with a zigzag edge to their blades, designed to cut fabric so that it will not fray. They make an attractive border to paper and card. They are not absolutely essential and a similar effect can be made by cutting zigzags by hand with small scissors – or just make a straight cut with ordinary scissors.

Scissors

Have two pairs of scissors – a large pair with long blades to enable you to make as few cuts as possible when cutting in a straight line, and a pair of small embroidery scissors to cut out holes and windows. To cut internal holes, pierce the centre of the piece you wish to remove with the point of the small scissors and cut out to the line carefully.

Do not use a valued pair of fabric shears *even once* for paper, as it blunts them very quickly.

Fabrics

Embroidery

For the one project in this book which requires a small piece of embroidery, I used an old embroidered handkerchief. These are available for pennies in a thrift shop or are very inexpensive to buy new,

and come in many lovely designs. If you prefer, you could look for an old embroidered table-cloth or something similar, from which you could cut a motif. (Take care not to cut up anything of antique value.) Wash and iron any items from thrift shops to make them easier to handle.

Hessian

Hessian is a rough woven material that is inexpensive and freely available from fabric shops and upholsterers, but you could probably beg an old hessian sack from your local pet shop or garden centre.

Knitted Fabric

A single motif from an old knitted jumper is required for each of the two knitwear projects (nos. 5 and 6). If you do not have something suitable in your wardrobe, go to thrift shops or jumble sales. It should be possible to get an adult's or child's jumper very cheaply, which will supply enough material for several cards.

Printed Christmas Fabric

There are many cottons printed with Christmas motifs, either with a white background or with deep-coloured backgrounds. Use whatever you like. I have used one with a white background. These specialist materials are more likely to be freely available around Christmas time, both in fabric shops and in craft shops.

Ribbons

Ribbons can be bought in any fabric shop and come in many widths and colours. There are also wide non-woven ribbons for sale in florists' which can be split down to the size you want by snipping the end and pulling the two halves apart. Florists also have ribbons with greetings printed on them, which are useful. None of these types of ribbon is very dear.

Miscellaneous

Correction Fluid

This is sold in stationers' for correcting typing, and covers printing with an opaque layer of white which can be written or typed over. If possible use the sort which is like a pen rather than the sort in a bottle, which tends to be less controllable.

Leaves

Pick fresh leaves for some projects and try using the veined side for a clear imprint. Use each fresh leaf only once as they are too fragile to use again. For dried leaves press undamaged, freshly picked leaves between blotting paper, or newspaper, under a weight for a few weeks to dry. Alternatively, whole bay leaves, which are a culinary herb, can be found in most grocers' shops and supermarkets.

Masking Tape

This is a sticky tape which can be repositioned and, if used with care, will not damage the paper it is stuck to. It is used whenever it is important to keep something in place.

Pictures To Copy

Calendars and postcards are abundant nearly everywhere and have pleasant scenes which are easily copied to form

the basis of the 'Photocopy and Wash' project. You could also use a picture from a magazine. The original size of the picture is unimportant as you will be using a photocopier to reduce or enlarge it to fit your card. If you wish to make this card without a photocopier, then the picture will have to be the right size for the card – i.e. smaller than A5, which is the size of an A4 sheet folded in half.

Sequins

Sequins come in many colours and are available in most shops that sell sewing accessories. They can be bought separately or in stitched strips like ribbon which are easy to take apart to get at the individual sequins.

Stamps and Embossing Powder

There is a lot of enthusiasm for art stamping at present, and consequently more and more shops are selling the equipment. Many toy shops and stationers have sets of small stamps and ink pads, and most hobby and art shops have larger, more sophisticated stamps with a greater range of accessories.

Embossing powder is a substance that, when scattered onto a newly printed image, sticks and can then be heated to produce a raised effect. The heat source can be either a cooker ring, a toaster or a heat gun, but for ease of use and safety the toaster is probably best. (A heat gun

is like a hairdryer without the fan, and is used for various do-it-yourself jobs such as paint-stripping.)

Sponge

Small natural sponges for applying make-up can be found in most chemists'. A cheaper alternative would be to cut up or pull apart an old car-washing or bath sponge to the desired size, which is roughly the size of a walnut.

Weights

In many of the projects in this book you are recommended to put work under a weight while the glue dries. You can make a suitable weight simply by enclosing a heavy book like a dictionary or encyclopaedia in a plastic bag so that it is protected from glue and paint.

Paint

Colour Mixing

In each project I have specified the colours you will need and how to mix them, but here I would just like to remind you of how to get different colours from the three primary colours: red, blue and yellow. With these three colours, and black and white for darker or lighter tones, you can create everything else you will ever need.

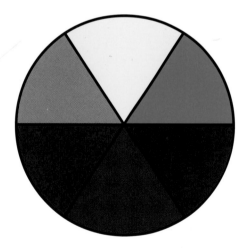

As I am sure you know,

● red and yellow mixed in equal parts make orange – more red makes a reddish orange, more yellow a yellowish orange;

● red and blue mixed in equal parts make purple – more red makes a reddish purple and more blue a bluish purple;

● blue and yellow mixed in equal parts make green – more blue makes a bluish green and more yellow makes a yellowish green.

By adding white to any of the above you will produce pastel shades, and small amounts of black darken the colours. The exception to this is water-colour, where adding more water, which allows more

white paper to show through, makes paler shades. Thicker paint, obscuring the white paper, makes darker shades. I have included a colour wheel for easy reference as a reminder of how the primary colours can be mixed. It is, of course, possible to buy every conceivable colour ready to use, but more satisfying, I think, to learn to mix them.

Water-Colour

It is possible to buy water-colour paints in jars, tubes, or pans – which are solid blocks of pigment which you rub with a wet brush to get the paint – very similar to children's paint sets. Water-colours have lovely colours and are a pleasure to use. However, they are expensive, as they are made from expensive materials which will not fade and will give true hues.

Children's painting sets also contain pans of water-colours, but are a fraction

Colour wheel. Between each pair of primary colours you will find the secondary colour obtained by mixing them of the price as they are poorer in quality. However, their colours are very good and they come in an almost infinite variety of shades. They are quite good enough for any of the projects in this book and you can always pass them on to your youngsters afterwards.

CAUTION Do not pass your expensive water-colours on to young children when you have finished with them, as many of them are poisonous.

Acrylic

This is my favourite medium and I have used it extensively throughout this book. This does not mean that it is the only paint which can be used – just that I find it suits me. It comes in tubes and pots and it seems to have endless uses. Watered down, it is as good as any water-colour, and has the advantage that, once dry, wetting will not smudge it – so creating a quality as permanent as printing. Acrylic can also be used on almost any surface – it will stick to glass, can be used on fabric and any paper surface. If you wish to dye fabric for a project (not for wear) a very dilute mix of acrylic will do this for you. Used very thickly you can produce a 3D surface which can be scraped into.

One of the advantages (and drawbacks) of acrylic is that it dries very quickly, and care has to be taken that a colour you have mixed does not dry out before you have finished using it. This can be avoided by mixing plenty of paint and by watching it and adding a little water if it seems to be thickening. This same quality can be very useful as it means that you can paint over previously painted sections quickly without creating a muddy mixture. This allows you to darken shades that are not quite right, or change the colour entirely.

TIP Some artists who use acrylics store their brushes lying permanently in water in a tray like a decorating-roller tray so as to avoid the bristles drying with any paint in them and becoming rigid and ruined.

CAUTION Unlike water-colour, once dry, acrylic is permanent – so it is wise to protect clothes, carpets etc. Read labels – some acrylics are toxic.

Emulsion

Silk-finish and matt emulsions are basically acrylics, and most of the above applies to them – although nearly all emulsions have a very large percentage of white in them, which limits their usefulness. Small pots for testing the colour are now available in most painting and decorating shops, and these give more than enough paint for most projects. Some even come with their own brush in the lid. They have a particularly nice texture which makes them useful for printing projects, as they are thick enough to stick to the surface of printing blocks without clogging them (see Project 17: Potato Print).

CAUTION Although these paints do not have a strong smell, some fumes may upset you – ventilate your work space.

Paint Tray and Pad

For some cards you are going to need a printing pad, which can be made by cutting a thin kitchen sponge-cloth to the size of any shallow dish or tray and saturating it with your chosen paint. This will prevent too much paint being deposited on the stamp. This is an alternative to painting the surface of the stamp before each print with paint on a paintbrush and, as you can imagine, is quite a bit quicker if a large number of prints is being undertaken.

Brushes

You will need a water-colour brush – while it is not necessary to buy a very high-quality brush, you should steer clear of very cheap ones. Choose a brush that

comes naturally to a point when wet and has bristles no thinner at the thickest part than a pencil, preferably slightly thicker.

A stiffer-bristled brush, such as a 6mm house-painting brush, is useful for painting larger areas, for putting paint on stamps, or for glue. Glue can also be put on with old brushes, spatulas or pieces of stiff card used as spreaders.

Pens and Pencils

Pencil and Rubber

Pencils are graded for hardness by letters and numbers. The HB pencil most of us used at school is medium – neither hard nor soft. The softest pencil is 6B and the hardest is 6H. A soft drawing pencil (4B or 5B) marks the paper or card without causing a dent, which erasing will not remove, and rubs out easily. These pencils are not very expensive and will last a long time with a little care. Try not to drop your pencil as this shatters the lead inside it so that it cannot be sharpened. One 4B or 5B pencil can be used wherever needed in all the projects in this book.

Buy an India rubber – not a plastic eraser as they are hard and can damage the paper surface. Keep your India rubber in the dark and it will stay soft and work well for you. Avoid erasing over a bigger area than is absolutely necessary, as it may affect the surface of the card or paper.

Felt-Tipped and Fibre-Tipped Pens

To make all the cards in this book you will need:

- **A thin, black, permanent pen** for tracing on plastic.
- **A very thick, black pen** for filling in the black lettering on the 'Merry Xmas' project. A thinner pen will work for this but will take far longer.
- **A variety of coloured pens** Buy a pack of 6, 12 or 24 coloured felt pens, which are sold for children to colour in with, to give you enough colours for all your needs.
- **A red felt pen** If you do not have the above you will need a red felt pen for the 'Happy Birthday' project (no. 9).
- **A gold marker** for greetings messages throughout the book, particularly for

writing on black or very dark cards. It could also be used to ink the block for the 'String Block Repeat'.

Templates and Other Aids

L-Shaped Framing Pieces

Make two L-shaped pieces out of thick card from a cardboard box and paint them black (or make them from black card). The inner measurements of the angles are the same as the measurements of A5 paper. Use them when you are selecting just part of a bigger picture to use. By holding them together you form a frame and mask the rest of what you are looking at. In this way the best part of a larger picture can be selected for use. The L-pieces can be seen in use in the illustrations to projects 13 and 15.

Master Templates

These are made from two A4 sheets of plain paper or card. Mark one A, and fold the other in half once (as illustrated), then carefully tear or cut along the fold. Mark one piece B and fold the other piece in half again. Cut or tear along the fold and, marking one piece C, fold the other in half and cut or tear along the fold. Mark one of the two remaining pieces D,

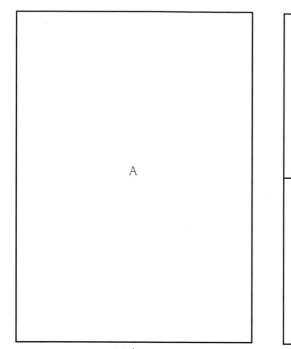

A4 sheet

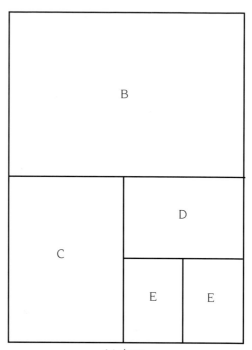

A4 sheet

halve the other piece once more and label both halves E. For some cards you will need several of these templates and they will get damaged, so make several at the beginning of the project. They will help you to cut paper and fabrics to size easily. Individual project instructions state whether to make the templates in card or paper.

Heart

In the instructions for projects 7 and 12 I have included full-sized heart patterns which you can trace and use – or you can make a heart template as follows. Any heart you cut out of your card has to be well within its margins so as not to

weaken the card. Take template C and fold it in half lengthways, long sides together. With a pencil, draw a half-heart design similar to those in the full-sized illustrations, beginning and ending at the folded edge. Try to keep the heart fat, and redraw until you are happy with the design. Then cut along the line of the half-heart. When you open out the paper you will have a symmetrical heart shape. You can now draw around this onto your card quite easily.

Full-Size Patterns

For some cards, a full-size pattern is included at the end of the instructions.

Greetings and Messages

What to Write

You will, I am sure, want to add messages to many of your own cards. There are three basic categories of message. The first are the obvious greetings like 'Merry Christmas' and 'Happy Birthday', which are self-explanatory. Second are the purely personal messages which I am sure you do not need my advice on. Lastly, there are verses and rhymes relevant to the themes of the cards, which many commercial cards include.

Care must be taken when borrowing poems from books for your own use. Traditional verses like 'Roses are red, Violets are blue, Sugar is sweet, And so are you' may not be to your taste, but along with nursery rhymes they are unattributed to any author and generally considered public property, so they are safe to use in your cards. Likewise, anyone quoting Shakespeare is unlikely to run into trouble. However, I would suggest that if you are planning to produce any cards for sale you use only your own poems, or verse which you have gained permission to use.

How to Write it

You may already know what you want to write but be concerned about how you can write it and make it look attractive. You may have decided to make the 'Happy Birthday' card but fear that your writing will spoil it, or similarly that your written greeting will mar a different attractively made card.

There are many ways around this problem. If you genuinely have an untidy hand you could try to improve it by getting a calligraphy set, or book, and learning to do one of the stylized scripts

Script or copperplate

Italic (sometimes called gothic)

Plain or sans-serif

Stencilled

they teach. Why not study different styles of writing and practice them to use on cards? I have included a few different alphabets for you to refer to.

You could give up trying to produce script yourself and use some aid to help you. Draughtsmen use stencils to make the lettering on plans; these are available in most art shops and stationers, and come in a variety of sizes which will suit most projects.

Many office suppliers', stationers' and art shops sell rub-down lettering sets, which come in a vast array of different styles and sizes. These sets consist of sheets of see-through plastic with lettering printed on them. You select each letter individually and, having positioned it over where you want it to be (for instance on the front of a card), you rub the back with a pencil or fingernail. The rubbing releases the letter

from the backing and sticks it to the card. You then position the next letter beside the first and thus build up words. The whole process takes longer to describe than to do and gives consistently good results.

Another source of legible lettering in varied sizes and styles is the word processor or computer. If you do not have one yourself, perhaps a friend could print out the words you need, and these can then be pasted into a card.

Why not use single letters cut from newspapers for your messages after the style of ransom notes and use this as a feature of the card's design?

Finally, any shop that sells rubber stamps for art projects will probably have a range of stamps of the more common messages – or buy a do-it-yourself office rubber-stamp kit from a stationer's and create short messages as you need them.

Making your own Envelopes

With the exception of the bought window cards, which come with their own envelopes, all the projects in this book are suitable for bought C5 envelopes. These come in brown, white and a limited range of colours, and so can be matched to some extent to the cards which will go in them if you wish. I tend to use only white.

When you decide to make a card with different proportions, or when you want to have an envelope of a particular material, you will need to make the envelope yourself. It is quite easy to make your own envelopes and these can be made in many different materials – coloured papers, brown wrapping paper, special occasion wrapping paper (such as Christmas or birthday designs) – although you may need to use a white label on a patterned or dark envelope to make the address legible.

If you do not wish to make your own envelopes but would like to make smaller cards, then find the envelope first and make your card to fit it. This is by far the easiest way.

Do not forget that any printed pattern you have put on your card can be put on the envelope too, if you wish, provided it is done in a medium that will not run if delivered in the rain.

Included here are two main basic envelopes, as you will see from the illustrations. Both designs are dependent on

the size of the cards which will go in them for their finished dimensions. Initially it may seem rather fiddly to make either style of envelope, but once you have tried it you will see that all that is needed is careful measuring for a good result.

If you intend to make more than one card the same size it is well worth making a durable template out of firm card or flat plastic so that after the initial measuring an envelope can be prepared quickly at any time by drawing around the template and cutting out.

Materials for Envelope Patterns

Scrap Paper Large sheets.
Card and Plastic Sheets Material from cereal boxes, or large ice-cream-tub lids, will do if the envelope does not have to be too big. For big envelopes use any firm material which you will be able to draw around when cut out, e.g. card from cardboard boxes.
Scissors Small scissors will be easiest to use here.
Felt Pen Black.
Ruler This must have centimetres marked on it.

If only one envelope is required, follow instructions as below but, instead of making the patterns, draw directly onto the back of your chosen paper in pencil.

Method Envelope I

Envelope I is the less complicated of the two designs and is made in the following way:

1 Place your greetings card centrally on a large sheet of scrap paper.

2 Draw round it carefully with pencil and remove the card.

3 On two sides only – bottom and right – measure and mark 1cm outside the line drawn round the card. Do this in two places and, positioning the ruler on both marks, draw a line parallel to the original.

4 Extend the new lines to form a new rectangle.

5 On left, right and top of the new rectangle measure and draw lines 2cm from the existing lines.

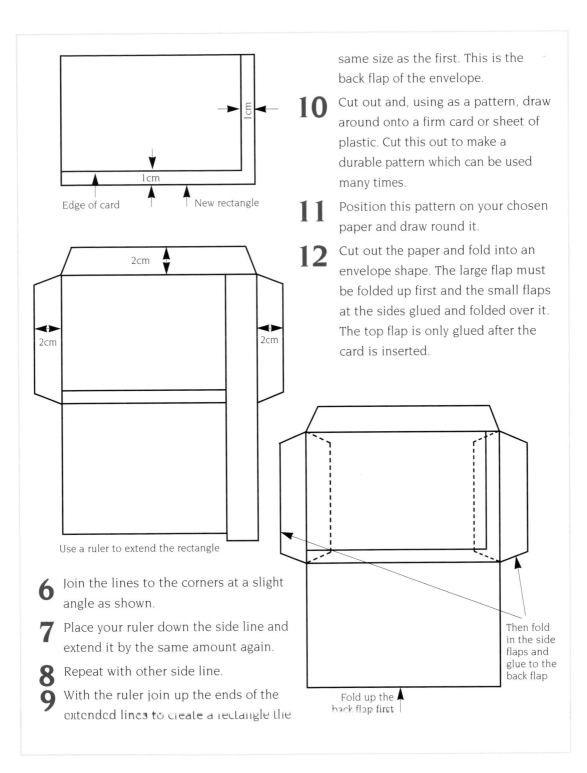

Edge of card   New rectangle

Use a ruler to extend the rectangle

same size as the first. This is the back flap of the envelope.

10 Cut out and, using as a pattern, draw around onto a firm card or sheet of plastic. Cut this out to make a durable pattern which can be used many times.

11 Position this pattern on your chosen paper and draw round it.

12 Cut out the paper and fold into an envelope shape. The large flap must be folded up first and the small flaps at the sides glued and folded over it. The top flap is only glued after the card is inserted.

6 Join the lines to the corners at a slight angle as shown.

7 Place your ruler down the side line and extend it by the same amount again.

8 Repeat with other side line.

9 With the ruler join up the ends of the extended lines to create a rectangle the

Then fold in the side flaps and glue to the back flap

Fold up the back flap first

Method
Envelope II

1 Place your card centrally on a large sheet of scrap paper.

2 Draw round it with a pen and remove the card.

3 On two sides only – bottom and right – measure and mark 1cm outside the line drawn round the card, as before.

4 Extend the new lines to form a new rectangle, as before.

5 Measure the width and depth of the new rectangle.

6 Measure out from the middle of the two sides in turn to two-thirds of the length of the rectangle, marking each point with a dot.

7 Measure out from the middle of the top and bottom in turn to two-thirds of the height of the rectangle, marking each point with a dot as before.

8 Lay your ruler along the top line of the rectangle and extend it at each end by 1cm.

9 Lay your ruler along the bottom line and extend it at each end by 1cm.

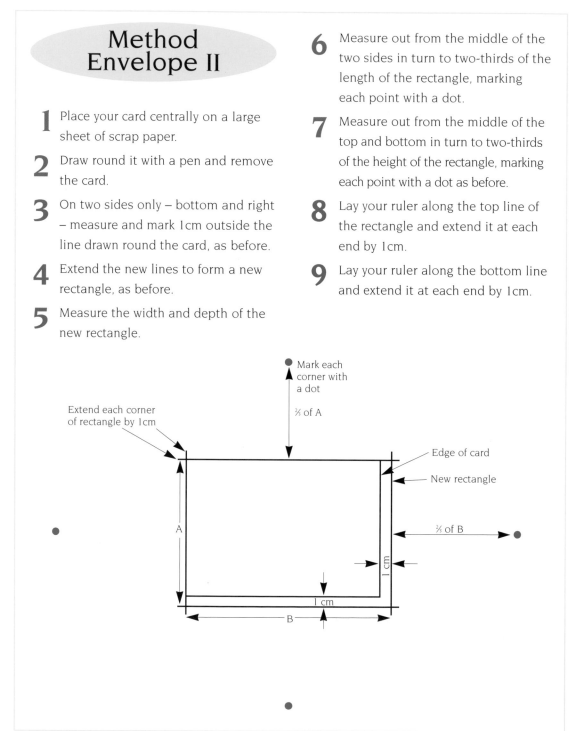

Mark each corner with a dot

⅔ of A

Extend each corner of rectangle by 1cm

Edge of card

New rectangle

A

⅔ of B

1 cm

1 cm

B

Join the dots to the
extended corners
of the rectangle

10 Lay your ruler along the left-hand line
and extend it at each end by 1cm.

11 Lay your ruler along the right-hand
line and extend it at each end by 1cm.

12 Join the ends of these lines to the
points you marked before to make
triangular extensions on each side
of the rectangle.

13 Cut out and use as a template to
make a durable pattern out of firm
card, as before.

14 Draw around the card pattern onto
your chosen paper and cut out.

15 The two side flaps fold in and the
bottom flap folds up over them and
is glued.

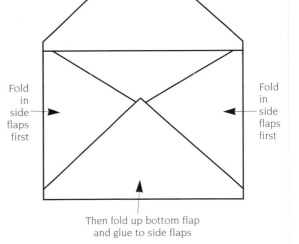

Fold
in
side
flaps
first

Fold
in
side
flaps
first

Then fold up bottom flap
and glue to side flaps

16 The top flap will be folded over after
the card is inserted and glued in
place or tucked in.

Gluing Projects

Here are four simple
and effective
projects which
require no special
materials or skills.
In each, paper
or fabric is
cut out and
glued into position on a card. The finished results
are quite different but equally successful.

1 Natural Collage
2 Christmas Layers
3 A Misty Scene in Tissue
4 'Congratulations'

1 Natural Collage

This project uses dried leaves and hessian in muted shades to produce a card which echoes current fashions in interior design and other areas, for a simple natural effect.

Materials

Card 1 x A4 sheet of photocopier card, buff or cream.

Glue Pritt Stick, Copydex or repositionable adhesive spray, and double-sided sticky tape are all fine for this card. I have used Pritt Stick and double-sided sticky tape throughout, but you should use what you wish.

Scissors Large scissors, or craft knife if you like to use it.

Fabric Hessian or sacking, not less than a 15cm square.

Paper Some brown wrapping paper or a brown-paper bag.

Leaves Dried, pressed leaves from your garden in a variety of sizes no more than 7cm or 8cm long, or a packet of bay leaves from your grocer. If you choose to use your own dried leaves these will have to be prepared some weeks in advance (see Materials and Techniques: Miscellaneous).

Templates C and E Described in Materials and Techniques. Cut two of C and one of E from paper.

Weight Use a heavy book such as a dictionary, in a plastic bag to protect it from paint and glue.

Pencil and Rubber

Method

1 Using template C, mark and cut out a rectangle of hessian, either by drawing round the template and cutting out or by holding the template steady with one hand and cutting along its sides through the hessian. Try to cut in line with the threads.

2 Carefully fray all four edges of the hessian rectangle by removing threads one at a time from each side in turn until 1cm of fringe is made all round.

3 Take the A4 card and fold it in half, putting the narrower sides together.

4 Lay the card on your work surface with the opening to the right.

5 Position a new template C centrally on the front of your folded card and put a light pencil mark at each corner to help you gauge where you will need to glue the card. As you will notice, the hessian does not have corners, as such, any more, but these marks will still indicate where the glue has to go.

6 Glue your card front all over the rectangular area defined by the four pencil marks, but try not to get glue on the pencil marks as this would seal them and prevent them being rubbed out later.

7 Carefully position the hessian onto the glued surface and smooth down. Smooth out the fringe onto the glued surface from the centre of the hessian to make sure it is attached and straight. You may be able to peel off the hessian and reglue if it is wrongly positioned, but slight mispositioning can be left as it adds to the handmade look .

8 Using template E as a guide, cut out a rectangle of brown paper, either by drawing around it onto the brown paper or by cutting around the template directly.

9 Some brown papers have quite different surfaces on either side. If this is the case with yours, select the side you wish to be visible and spread glue on the reverse. If there is no difference simply glue one side.

10 Stick the brown paper rectangle centrally on the hessian. It does not have to be too precisely central. Because the hessian is rough, smooth the paper on and put a weight on top until it is stuck firmly and the glue is dry.

11 While you wait for the brown paper to stick, select the leaves you wish to use. Choose three or four whole leaves in varying sizes.

12 Position your leaves on the brown paper so that they stick over the edge a little onto the hessian. Refer to the picture of the completed card if you are not sure.

13 When you are happy with the arrangement, stick the leaves onto

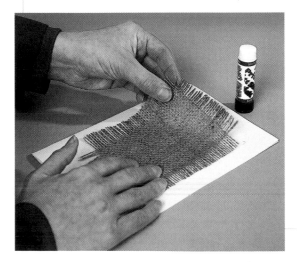

the brown paper. It is possible to glue them, weighting them afterwards until dry, but it is much simpler to put a small strip of double-sided sticky tape onto the back of each leaf and then stick down, particularly if the leaves are dry and fragile.

14 When all is dry rub out your guiding pencil marks.

15 Leave this card blank as a notelet or write a personal message inside; see Greetings and Messages.

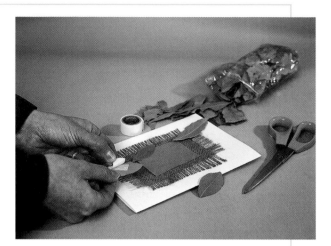

Variations

Vary the size of this card by using A5 card and reducing the size of each layer. A very small card would look wonderful, made in the same way but with one single leaf central on it. The whole look of this project would be altered by changing the types of material and paper – perhaps silks and handmade papers topped with beads or buttons in place of the leaves. Or use gold-painted leaves for a luxurious look.

2 Christmas Layers

'Christmas Layers' uses similar techniques to 'Natural Collage', i.e. layering of contrasting materials, to create an individual and attractive Christmas greeting card for someone special.

Materials

Card 1 x A4 sheet of photocopier card, red.
Glue Pritt Stick, Copydex or reposi-tionable adhesive spray, and double-sided sticky tape.
Scissors Large scissors and pinking shears, or a craft knife if you like to use it.
Fabric You will need some cotton with a small Christmas motif on a white, red or green background. Start with at least a 15cm square.
Foil New roasting foil that has been crumpled and smoothed out to give some texture, or used, washed foil which has been smoothed out.
Tinsel You will need a piece of tinsel 2cm less than the long side of the D template. If it is very thin you should use twice as much, folded in half. Choose a colour that tones with your card and fabric, probably red or green, or something metallic like gold or silver.
Pencil
Templates C and D Cut two of C and one of D from paper.

Method

1 Fold the A4 photocopier card in half, putting the narrower sides together.

2 Lay the card on your work surface with the opening to the right.

3 Lay template C on the fabric and mark round it with the pencil; then cut out the rectangle of fabric with pinking shears.

4 Position a second template C centrally on the front of your folded card so that one of its narrower sides is to the top, and put a pencil mark on the card at each corner of the template to help you position your fabric.

5 Glue the card front all over the rectangular area defined by the four pencil marks, but try not to cover the pencil marks as this will prevent you rubbing them out.

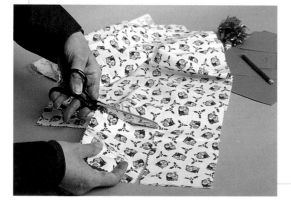

6 Carefully position the fabric onto the glued surface and smooth down. Make sure the pinked edges are glued down.

7 Using template D and the pencil, mark and cut out a rectangle of foil.

8 Foils have quite different surfaces on either side, one dull and one shiny, so select the side you wish to be visible and carefully spread glue on the reverse.

9 Stick the foil rectangle centrally on the fabric. This does not have to be too precisely central. Allow the glue to dry.

10 Now attach the tinsel to the centre of the foil. It is possible to glue it, but this can be rather messy. It is much simpler to cut a strip of double-sided sticky tape approximately the length of the tinsel and, removing its backing paper, stick down the tinsel upright onto the tin-foil rectangle.

11 Write a Christmas message inside.

Variations

Make this card smaller, or instead of foil and tinsel layer the Christmas fabric with a ribbon which has a greeting printed on it, available from florists. Frame the design on either card with thin tinsel.

3 A Misty Scene in Tissue

The effect here is created by the layering of the tissue paper, which creates different tones, the depth of the colour being dictated by the number of layers of tissue on each part of the scene.

Materials

Card 1 x A4 sheet of photocopier card, white.

Glue PVA glue diluted with equal parts of water and stirred well. (In this case this is the only glue which is suitable.)

Ruler or any straightedge.

Scissors Large and small. A craft knife is not really suitable for this project.

Tissue You will need part of a packet of blue tissue, the more translucent the better.

Felt Pen Black or grey. The sort of pen which is designed for children to colour with, and is just a little thick for writing, is ideal for this, and should be wide enough to hide any irregularities in your work. Alternatively:

Ribbon Very thin grey or black ribbon is an optional alternative to the felt pen as you will see in the text.

Template C One made out of card and several made out of photocopy paper.

Scrap Paper Newspaper to protect various surfaces.

Paper Clips

Pencil

Pattern The full-size pattern for this card can be found at the end of the instructions. You will need to make one complete copy or tracing of it, and a second copy which need include only the outline and line 5.

Method

1. You are going to need five layers of tissue the size of template C. Smooth out a sheet of tissue on your work surface and position the card template C in the bottom left-hand corner so that two sides line up with the sides of the tissue.

2. Draw round the other two sides.

3. Move the template up the edge of the tissue, lining it up with the side of the tissue and the line of the previous rectangle. Draw round the other two sides.

4 Repeat this process, lining the template up with the edge of the paper and the last rectangle drawn, until you have five rectangles drawn.

5 Carefully cut out all five rectangles with your large scissors, making as few cuts as possible along the sides so that the rectangles have a smooth edge.

6 Take a paper copy of template C and copy the design of the full-size pattern onto it. This does not have to be perfect, but if you do not wish to copy the lines freehand then trace through the paper of the template by placing it on top of the illustration. The paper is thin enough for you to be able to see strong lines like these through it.

7 Put one of your tissue rectangles aside, as it will be stuck on whole; this is piece A.

8 Put another tissue rectangle beneath your traced design, matching the edges. Paper-clip together half-way down the sides. Make sure the paper clips do not cover line 1.

9 Cut along line 1. The smaller scissors will help you cut around the curves better.

10 Take off the paper clips. Retain the bottom piece of tissue paper, which is piece B, and discard the top piece.

11 Clip the template to the next rectangle of tissue, lining up the bottom edge. Cut along line 2 with the small scissors to make piece C.

12 Repeat this process, clipping the tissue to the tracing and cutting along lines 3 and 4, to make pieces D and E. Each time retain the bottom piece of tissue and discard the top.

13 Carefully lay out the pieces of tissue paper in order.

14 Take the two tissue layers B and C and lay them on top of each other, the larger at the back, matching up the bottom edges. Take your second pattern which has line 5 marked on it, and lay it over the two pieces of tissue, matching bottom edges.

15 Cut along line 5 and retain the top parts of the pieces of tissue, discarding the bottom parts.

16 Using the original plan of the design to help with the positioning, lay out all the tissue pieces to see the effect you are trying to achieve. The top of the picture will be one layer thick and the other areas will vary from one layer to three.

17 Fold the A4 photocopy card in half, putting the narrower sides together.

18 Lay the card on your work surface with the opening to the right.

19 Position a fresh template C on the front of the card and centralize it. With a pencil, mark the card with small dots at each corner of the paper to mark its position.

20 Shut the card over a sheet of news-paper to protect the back. Paint over the marked rectangle with dilute PVA.

21 Position the full-sized tissue rectangle (piece A) onto the card within the pencil marks and glue, smoothing it over with the glue brush. This will lay down quite enough glue to stick the next layer. Smooth well, but most wrinkles will disappear as the paper dries.

22 Smooth down the two bottom layers (D and E) next, lining up the bottom edges, and smooth over with the glue brush. Paint a layer of glue over the whole tissue area, which will lay down enough glue for the next layer.

23 Using the plan of the picture to help you, lay down piece B and smooth with the glue brush as before.

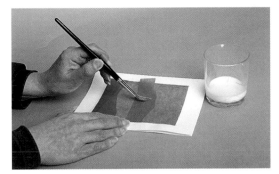

24 Line up the bottom of the last piece of tissue (C) with the bottom of piece B and glue in place.

25 The glue on the card front may make it curl and spoil all your hard work, so now you must 'varnish' both the inside and outside with a layer of PVA glue to stabilize the card and stop it curling. Do not worry that it curls when it is wet – it will be all right when it is dry.

26 Lay the card open on the work surface with the outside uppermost. Cover the whole top surface of the card with a thin layer of glue to seal. Allow to dry. The card may well curl while it is drying but this will correct itself when the other side is done.

27 Now turn the card over and paint the whole of the inside with a layer of PVA.

28 Allow to dry thoroughly, then refold and cover the whole of the card with scrap paper and press under your prepared weight for a few hours to ensure that it remains flat.

29 With the grey or black felt pen and a ruler, carefully draw a line around the outer edge of the tissue picture to frame it.

30 If you do not feel confident to draw this line, or feel that the edges need to be concealed more because they are too irregular, then stick the thin ribbon in place over the edges of the tissue. Cut four strips of ribbon, two the length of the short sides of the picture and two the length of the long sides, then put a thin line of glue around the edge of the tissue and stick down first the long sides and then the short. You may have to put an extra dab of glue at the corners where the ribbons overlap.

31 Leave this card blank to use as a notelet or write a message inside.

Variations

Try using different colours of tissue for different effects, and vary the type of landscape from very flat with trees to very mountainous.

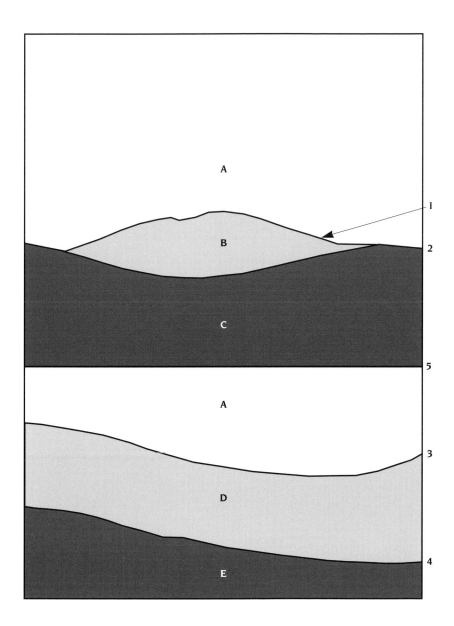

Full-size pattern for Project 3

4 'Congratulations'

The bold image of a champagne bottle combines with the sparkle of sequins and gold writing to suggest a festive occasion in this fun card. The quality of the finished card will depend greatly on the care which is taken with the cutting out and gluing.

Materials

Card 1 x A4 sheet of photocopier card, white.

Glue PVA or Pritt Stick.

Scissors Small scissors, or a craft knife if you prefer.

Sequins You will need about a dozen silver or gold sequins.

Picture of a Champagne Bottle You will need a picture from a magazine of a champagne or sparkling wine bottle approximately 10–15cm high. Sunday supplements are a good source, as are supermarkets' own magazines or any food magazine. If you cannot find one the right size, take whatever sized picture you can find to the local photo-copying shop and get them to enlarge or reduce it. Use a sparkling wine bottle if champagne proves too hard to find.

Confetti The tissue-paper, multicoloured kind. You will only need a handful.

Felt Pen Gold.

Method

1 Fold the A4 photocopier card in half with narrow sides together.

2 Lay the card on your work surface, open side to the right.

3 Put some scrap paper inside the card to protect the back from glue.

4 Having selected your picture of a bottle of champagne or wine, cut it out, remembering to remove the top of the cork so that it looks as if it has been opened.

5 Arrange the bottle on the card as per the photograph and mark its position lightly with a pencil. The bottle should come at least half-way up the card at an angle from the bottom right-hand corner.

39

6 Put the cut-out bottle face down on some scrap paper, spread glue over the back of it and stick it in place, leaving any excess bottle overhanging the edge of the card. This will be cut off when the glue is dry.

7 Once the glue is dry, trim the excess bottle off by cutting with scissors carefully along the edges of the card.

8 With the gold pen write 'Congratulations!' across the top of the card and draw in the lines at the neck of the bottle, as shown, to indicate that the cork has burst from the bottle.

9 Arrange the sequins around the card like bubbles bursting from the bottle, and when you are happy with their positioning glue them down individually.

10 When the card is completely dry, write your personal message inside and before putting it into the envelope place a handful of confetti inside for a surprise when it is opened.

Variations

The same card could be used with different messages such as 'It's a Boy!', 'Best Wishes for your Retirement', 'You've Passed your Test!'

Window Cards

Although two of these projects call for the more expensive ready-made window cards, both use discarded textiles, which keep the final price down and are an enjoyable way to recycle.

5 Knitwear Project I

Fair Isle knitting, with its ornate patterns and beautiful colour combinations, is the starting-point for this attractive card. By framing a single motif you highlight its intricacy, creating a picture like a small Victorian sampler.

Materials

Patterned Knitwear Preferably Fair Isle or similar, with several colours and repeated motifs. For this project you will need to seek out a piece of waste knitwear from your wardrobe, a jumble sale or a thrift shop. It will not be expensive and will give you material for several cards.

Bought Window Card These come in a variety of sizes with envelopes. It is wise to find the knitwear first as you can then select a card with the correct size of window for the motif you intend to use. Take some time to see how these cards are put together before you start making the card, to avoid gluing the wrong flaps.

Glue Pritt Stick or any glue that does not soak into the card. Test on scrap card before you use. It is also possible to use double-sided tape wherever glue is called for in this project, but if the knitting is thick the tape may not be strong enough to hold, so experiment. Weighting the card for a while can help secure glue or tape.

Felt-Tip Pen This is to mark the knitwear where necessary.

Scissors Large.

Scrap Paper Some sheets of newspaper.

Weight A heavy book, in a plastic bag to protect it from glue.

Method

1 Wash, if necessary, and press the piece of knitwear you have chosen.

2 Open out the window card and you will see that there are three sections. Grip the two outer sections, one in each hand, and hold so that the centre section with the window in it lies on the work surface.

3 Move the window over the knitwear, looking down through the window, until you find a motif you like and which fits the window well.

4 With one hand keep the window in place over the motif while with the

other you fold in the flaps so that the card is in its fully folded state.

5 Carefully put a dot with a felt-tip pen at each corner of the folded card. This is to guide you when you cut the motif out.

6 If you feel you need to draw a line with a ruler between the dots on the

knitwear to give you a rectangle to cut out, do so – or just cut from dot to dot with long scissors.

7 Open out the card and stick double-sided tape, or put a thick line of glue, around the window hole on the wrong side.

8 Put the cut square of knitting right side up on your table and, holding the card as before by the two outer flaps, lower the glued back of the card down onto the knitting, looking through the window to centralize the motif as you do so.

9 Let the flaps fall so that the card is flat on top of the knitting. Cover the whole with scrap paper and a weight and leave to stick firmly.

10 When the glue is completely firm, cut away the excess, unglued knitting so that you have a border of bare card to put glue, or tape, on to secure the window section of the card to its backing flap.

11 Put tape, or a thick line of glue, on all the bare card around the knitting and close its back flap onto the glue.

12 Insert scrap paper into the main opening of the card to protect the back, if necessary, and close. Put a weight on top, as before, until completely stuck.

13 This card is quite fat and may not fit into the envelope it came with. In this case use the envelope for something else and buy or make a bigger one for your card. See Making your own Envelopes.

14 Leave the card blank as a notelet, or if the knitted motif suggests a use to you (for example, a red and white motif might suggest Christmas), write in an appropriate message.

Variations

The greatest variations in this card can be produced by using different knitwear and setting it against different-coloured cards. Experiment.

6 Knitwear Project II

Humorous cards are always very popular and this one should produce a wry smile from its recipient. A pretty scrap of knitting will help to create a pleasing finished item. If you have already made Knitting Project I you will have plenty of scrap knitting to use.

Materials

Card 1 x A4 sheet of photocopier card, white.

Knitwear You can use up scraps from Knitwear Project I or use any piece of knitwear at least 12cm by 4cm. Try to make it an attractive piece.

Glue Pritt Stick, Copydex, PVA or double-sided sticky tape.

Scissors Small scissors are necessary to cut the window in this card.

Felt Pens A pack of multicoloured pens such as a child might have for colouring in. A black felt pen.

Pencil and Ruler

Template D Cut out in photocopier paper.

Scrap Paper You will need some newspaper for protecting areas, and a sheet of scrap white paper to make an extra template with.

Method

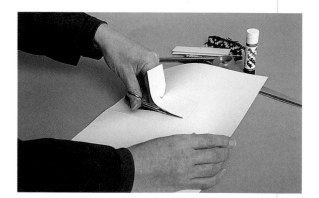

1 Fold the A4 card in half with its shorter sides together.

2 Lay the card on the work surface with the opening to the right.

3 Fold template D in half with its long sides together to make a tall, narrow rectangle and, using this new shape as the pattern, place it on the front of the card to the left of the middle.

4 Mark around the paper rectangle with a pencil and cut out with the small scissors by sticking the point in the centre of the marked area and cutting out to the lines. It is important that this should be neatly done, so take your time.

5 Press your piece of knitting.

6 Draw around the same long narrow rectangle of paper onto the white scrap paper and measure 1cm outside it all round. Draw this larger rectangle with the ruler. This will be a pattern to cut out your piece of knitting, which has to be large enough to fit behind the hole you have made.

7 Draw round the paper onto the knitting with a felt pen and cut out. If you are using a small offcut or test piece of

knitting you may decide to use it whole, provided it is larger than the hole and sufficiently smaller than the card to leave room to write your message.

8 With the card shut, take the pencil and draw around inside the window which you have already cut so that you mark its shape on the inside of the card.

9 Open the card and position the paper template which you used for cutting out the knitting on top of the rectangle you have marked. Draw round it with the pencil.

10 Thickly glue the whole of the larger rectangle.

11 Stick the knitting onto the glued area, smoothing it to make sure it is firm. Make this as neat as you can.

12 Check that when the card is shut you can see the knitting through the window, but that the edges are hidden.

13 Open the card and put scrap paper and then a weight onto the knitting until it is completely dry.

14 When the glue is dry, put the card down on the work surface, open, with the inside uppermost.

15 Inside, alongside the knitting, write the message 'THIS IS AS FAR AS I GOT!' using all the felt pens in turn so that nearly every letter is a different colour, repeating the colours as necessary.

16 Now close the card and next to the window write, in similar multicoloured irregular capitals, 'I WANTED TO MAKE YOU A JUMPER FOR YOUR BIRTHDAY BUT . . . .'

17 At the bottom of the inside page write 'HAPPY BIRTHDAY!' in black felt pen.

Variations

Adapt this card for different occasions without changing the basic design, for example 'I WANTED TO GET YOU A DESIGNER JUMPER FOR CHRISTMAS BUT . . . THIS IS ALL I COULD AFFORD!'

7 Pink Ribbon Valentine

A pink heart made of ribbon makes this romantic card special. Although simple to make, the finished card looks anything but home-made.

Materials

Card 1 x A4 sheet of photocopier card, white.

Glue PVA or double-sided tape.

Scissors Small scissors work well to cut out the heart and to cut the ribbon, but if you feel confident with a craft knife by all means use it.

Ribbon At least half-metre (50cm) lengths of at least three different widths and tones of pink ribbon. Do not use wider than 2cm.

Lace As you will see, I have used the gathered sort, but any narrow lace would be all right.

Felt Pens Gold or pink felt pens would be nice for writing your message inside.

Templates B and C One of each made out of photocopier card; both can be cut from the same A4 sheet of card.

Pencil 4B or 5B.

Method

1 Take the card template C and carefully fold it in half lengthways with long sides together.

2 With a pencil draw half a heart, starting and ending at the fold. If you are not satisfied first time, redraw. There is no need to rub out – this is only a template. You could make the template out of paper and trace the full-size heart pattern given at the end, if you wish. However, extra care would need to be taken when drawing round it, as it would be much flimsier than the card heart.

3 When you are happy with your drawing, cut it out, still folded, and then open to reveal the completed heart. Alternatively, cut out your tracing of the heart.

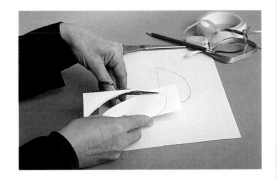

4 Take the sheet of A4 card and fold in half with the short sides together. Lay it on your work surface with opening to right.

5 Position the cut-out heart as centrally as possible on the front of the card.

6 Lightly draw round the heart with the pencil to transfer the shape to the card.

7 Open the card out flat to avoid cutting through the back layer as well. Cut out the heart-shaped opening, either by piercing in the middle with the scissors and carefully cutting outwards towards the line or by laying the card open on a cutting board or mat, and cutting carefully round with a sharp craft knife.

8 Enclose template B in your folded card and with the pencil mark any parts that protrude around the edge by drawing along the edge of the card.

9 Next draw around the inside of the heart cut-out so as to transfer its shape to the enclosed piece of card. It is important to do it this way so that any irregularities in your cutting out of the heart are transferred to the insert.

10 Take out the card insert and trim off any protruding edges which you marked in step 8. On the insert, either liberally glue the whole heart shape or stick double-sided tape right around the heart outside the pencil line. There is no need to follow the shape – a rectangle of tape will do fine.

11 Stick strips of ribbon horizontally across the glued heart area, starting in the centre with the widest piece and mixing the ribbons so that there are no two the same width or tone together.

12 Each time you stick down a piece of ribbon, cut off the excess.

13 When the insert is dry – or immediately, if you are using double-sided tape – enclose it in the card to check that the ribbons are visible through the hole. Then put glue or more double-sided tape right round the insert's outer edge and fix it in place.

14 Enclose scrap paper in the card to protect the back from glue, if necessary, and place under a weight until firmly glued.

15 Remove the weight and scrap paper, lay the card closed on the work surface.

16 Position the lace around one side of the cut-out heart from top middle to bottom middle to measure how much is needed.

17 Cut the lace to size and use it to cut another piece the same length for the other side of the heart.

18 Run a thin line of glue around the outside of the cut-out heart.

19 Glue down the two pieces of lace around the two sides of the cut-out heart. If using gathered lace, the fullness should be to the outside (see finished card).

20 Weight and leave to dry thoroughly.

21 If you wish, with a gold or pink felt pen write 'To my' above the heart and 'Valentine' below – or leave the front plain and put a personal message inside.

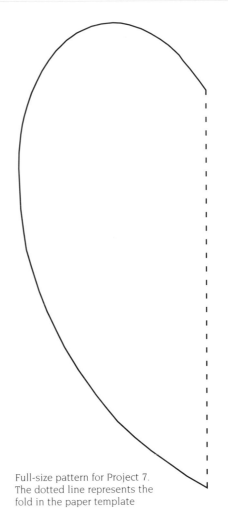

Full-size pattern for Project 7. The dotted line represents the fold in the paper template

Variations

Move away from tradition and make this card in another colour, perhaps lilac or red, or select a rainbow of coloured ribbons and use them in turn on the same card. Perhaps replace the lace with the outer part of a heart-shaped paper doily sprayed gold, or with the tiny embroidered flowers sold in fabric shops for appliquéing to blouse collars.

8 Found Embroidery

For many years it has been possible to buy greetings card kits which contain a tiny embroidery to stitch, along with a frame card and envelope. This project allows you to create the same effect even if you do not possess the embroidery skills.

Materials

Embroidery The starting-point of this card is a piece of embroidery from an old handkerchief or piece of table-linen. If you are using a handkerchief from a thrift shop then wash and iron it, as it is much easier to work with something which is not crumpled.

Card The bought window card will have to be selected to suit the size of the embroidery. If the material is old and not very white, do not choose a white card, as it will make the old fabric look more dingy. A far better choice would be a coloured card in one of the colours of the embroidery.

Glue Pritt Stick, Copydex or double-sided sticky tape.

Paper You will need one sheet of white photocopy paper to stick the fabric to for ease of handling.

Weight A heavy book such as a dictionary, put in a plastic bag to protect it from glue.

Pencil Soft, 2B–5B.

Scrap Paper Newspaper will be fine.

Method

1 Put the white paper under the closed card on your work surface, and with the pencil draw round it to get a piece of paper the same size as the card. Cut this out, cutting just inside the drawn line.

2 With the piece of paper closed inside the card where the insert has to go, mark through the window with the pencil.

3 If the embroidery is very near to the edge of the hanky you will need to create a border to stick into the card by having the paper sticking out around the hanky. The fabric will have to be positioned on the paper in such

a way that the embroidery is placed where it will be seen through the window with no edges showing. Mark the hanky when you are happy with the position.

4 Cover the paper insert with glue and position the fabric so that the embroidery is over the drawing of the window.

5 Allow to dry completely under a weight.

6 Cut away any fabric which protrudes beyond the edge of the paper.

7 Check the embroidery in the card to see that it appears in the window. Make any necessary adjustments by trimming the fabric and paper to fit.

8 Glue around the window on the inside of the card, or put double-sided tape around the window.

9 Put the fabric, right side up, flat on the work surface and, holding one of the outer flaps of the card in either hand, lower the window section onto the fabric. By looking through the hole you should be able to position it perfectly. See 'Knitting Project I' for an illustration of this method.

10 Let the flaps fall so that the card is flat on top of the fabric, and cover the whole thing with scrap paper and a weight until it is stuck.

11 Glue or tape the back section of the card onto the back of the fabric and paper insert.

12 Enclose a piece of waste paper in the card to protect the back from glue, if necessary, and weight until stuck again..

13 Leave this card blank to use as a notelet or for any occasion.

Variations

Variety in this card depends on what you are able to find in the way of embroidery. Look out for embroidered table-linen or worn tapestry cushions which have small areas worth saving. Recently, very cheap tie-dyed and hand-painted silk scarves have been coming into this country from China and any one of these would make several very attractive cards. Silk is thin, so it would be wise to keep the glue or tape to its edges in case it showed through the fabric.

Designing with Words

The written word is everywhere in our society. A walk down any high street displays a wealth of different written messages on shop signs, posters, hoardings, and street and traffic signs. Words are also easy to produce and, as you will see in the following four projects, they create an interesting all-over effect when repeated over a large area.

9 'Happy Birthday' Repeat

This is a card which conveys its message clearly and repeatedly. 'Happy Birthday' is reproduced over its entire front surface. The single phrase highlighted in red emphasizes the greeting and gives style to the card. There is no need to be concerned that your writing is not good enough for this project, as the repetition creates a charm of its own.

Materials

Card 1 x A4 photocopier card, white.
Pens Black and red felt pens for writing with – not too thin.

Photocopier (See instruction 9 for ways to make this card without the photocopier.)
Correction Fluid

Method

1 Study the picture of the finished card to see how the words run right off the edge of the card.

2 Fold the A4 card in half with the short sides together.

3 Lay the card on the work surface with its opening to the right.

4 Start writing in the top left-hand corner of the card with the 'Y' of 'BIRTHDAY' and write 'HAPPY BIRTHDAY' repeatedly across the card. If you find it difficult to write in straight lines, you may need to rule guidelines first.

5 Starting each line at a different position in the phrase, continue writing 'HAPPY BIRTHDAY' in lines across the page.

6 If you intend to photocopy the card, write the message all the way to the bottom and then use correction fluid to block out the 'HAPPY BIRTHDAY' which is in the most central position.

7 Photocopy the number of cards you want.

8 Then write 'HAPPY BIRTHDAY' in red felt pen in each space. This way you can be sure that the space you have left will exactly fit the words to go into it.

NOTE Some photocopiers leave a thin strip down the leading edge of the copy which is unprinted. Ask the copy-shop staff about this so that they can position the card in such a way that this does not

10 When you are finished, open the card and write 'HAPPY BIRTHDAY' in red across the inside right of the card in a similar central position to the red on the front.

Variations

This project could be made using a word processor (and colour printer if you have one). Experiment with the size of font. Either the word-processor or the photocopy version can be made in bulk. For the hand-written method try using a gold felt pen instead of the red one.

spoil your card front. If this cannot be avoided, ask them to use a guillotine to trim the unprinted edge from your card.

9 If you are only making one card and do not want to use a photocopier, write the central 'HAPPY BIRTHDAY' in red felt pen when you reach it. However, if you use the photocopy method you can then blank out whichever phrase you like after seeing the completed card front instead of having to make the decision when the writing is only half-way down the page.

10 'Merry Xmas'

This is a modern version of the traditional Christmas card. It does not need snow or reindeer to get its message across – the striking red and black colour scheme shouts it to the world. Two methods have been included for this card. In the first you can use the full-sized pattern to reproduce my design, but in Method II you have to design the front of the card for yourself. Have a go at both methods.

Materials

For both methods
Card 1 x A4 photocopier card, red.
Pens Thin and thick black felt pens.
Photocopier See 'Variations' for ways
to make this card without a photocopier.
Pencil, ruler and rubber

For Method I
Paper White photocopy paper, or
tracing paper and carbon paper.
Full-Sized Pattern for this card.
Masking Tape

For Method II
Templates Templates B and E in white
paper.

Instructions are included first for
using the pattern and secondly for
designing your own card.

Method I

1 Place the photocopy paper over the
full-sized pattern (securing it with
masking tape if you wish) and trace
the design for the front of the card
with the pencil.

2 Go over the outlines of the letters
with the thinner black felt pen.

3 Fill in the background to the letters
with the thicker pen.

4 Using a photocopier, copy this design
onto the red card so that when the
card is folded it forms the front.

5 Use the photocopier to make another
copy of the design, reduced to
approximately the size of template E.

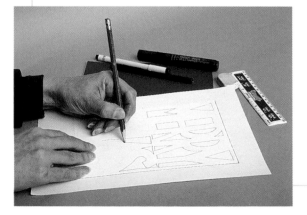

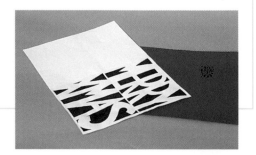

6 Position the reduced design in the photocopier so that when printed onto the red card it will be central on the inside, right-hand side of the card.

7 Fold the A4 card in half with the short sides together.

8 Add your personal message inside.

Method II

1 Fold template B in half with short sides together and open out.

2 Put template B on your work surface with a short side at the bottom and fold horizontally across the middle.

3 Mark the bottom half into four even sections. This is most easily done by folding.

4 With the ruler and pencil, mark the top half above the fold for five approximately even upright sections.

5 With the pencil draw in the letters for the greeting 'MERRY XMAS'. The letters are supposed to be large and squashed together. Do this quite lightly as you

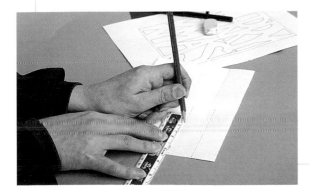

Variations

This card can be made without the aid of a photocopier by tracing or drawing the design and then laying the red card on the work surface with the opening to the right. With carbon paper and the tracing you made, transfer the design to the front of the card instead of template B. The inside motif can be made by drawing the whole design smaller on a red template E which can then be stuck inside the card – fiddly, but not impossible!

Vary this card for other occasions by using different words and different colours of card – for instance, a 'Happy Easter' card in green pen on yellow card (turning the card so that its widest side is to the bottom to fit), or 'Love you!' in two shades of pink on pink. A card made with the small 'Merry Xmas' (which is used inside this card) centred or repeated on the front would be a stylish variation.

may want to rub out a few times before you are happy with the layout.

6 With a ruler draw a narrow border right round the card front to frame it (see finished card).

7 Continue as for Method I, steps 2–8.

Full-size pattern for Project 10

HERE'S A CARD FULL OF **MONEY** FOR YOUR BIRTHDAY.

11 'Money'

In any card shop humorous birthday cards outnumber any other kind, and this one, while a trifle obvious, should cause its receiver a groan of appreciation.

Materials

Card 1 x A4 photocopier card, white or cream.
Felt Pen Gold or silver felt pen, and thin black felt pen.

Ribbon Thin gold ribbon. I have used florists' ribbon.
Glue Pritt Stick or PVA and a small brush.
Scrap Paper Newspaper.

Method

1 Fold the A4 card in half with short edges together.

2 Place the card on the work surface with opening to right.

3 Open the card out. You will be writing 'MONEY' in lines all over the right-hand half of the inside of the card using the gold pen.

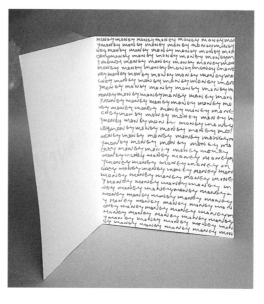

4 When writing 'MONEY', start each line of writing in a different place on the word so that the words do not form columns.

5 Leave the card open until the ink is dry, and then close and lay on the work surface with the opening to the right.

6 Following the layout shown and using the black and gold pens, write 'HERE'S A CARD FULL OF MONEY FOR YOUR BIRTHDAY!' on the front of the card.

7 When the ink is dry, insert a large piece of scrap paper into the card to protect it.

8 Cut two pieces of ribbon to fit along the two long sides of the card, and two pieces to fit along the two short sides.

9 Now run a thin line of glue around the edges of the card front.

10 Glue down the long strips of ribbon first and dab a little glue on the top and bottom ends of each where the other pieces of ribbon will overlap.

11 Now stick down the shorter lengths of ribbon, making sure that the ends are stuck on top of the ends of the long pieces.

NOTE your personal message will have to be written on the left-hand flap inside this card.

Variation

Design your own £10 or £20 note to the size of the A4 sheet of card and colour to resemble a real note with coloured pencils. Make a similar front for the card.

12 'I Love You' Valentine

All valentines are supposed to mean 'I love you', and this one says it clearly. The design is very simple but produces a very good finished article.

Materials

Card 1 x A4 photocopier card, white.
Felt Pens Red and pink.
Scissors Small scissors work well for cutting out the heart shapes; or use a craft knife if you prefer.
Template C One in photocopier card and one in photocopier paper.
Carbon Paper
Masking Tape
Scrap Paper
Full-Sized Pattern for heart.
Pencil and Rubber

Method

1 Take the paper template and with masking tape secure it over the full-size pattern of the heart. With the pencil trace the heart.

2 Place the tracing on top of the carbon paper, on top of the card template C. Secure with masking tape.

3 With the pencil retrace the heart, pressing heavily to make an impression on the card template.

onto the card. Keep this template to use again.

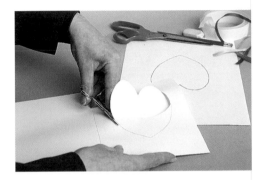

5 Take the sheet of A4 card and fold in half with short sides together.

6 Lay the card on your work surface with the opening to the right.

7 Position the cut-out heart as centrally as possible on the front of the card.

8 Lightly draw round the heart with the pencil to transfer the shape to the card.

9 Open out the card and cut out the heart, either by piercing in the middle with the scissors and carefully cutting out towards the line or by laying the

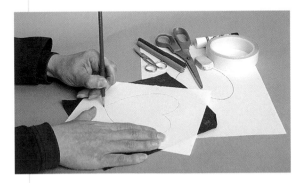

4 Cut out the card heart. Because it is stiffer than the paper it will be much easier to draw round it accurately

card open on a cutting board or mat and cutting carefully round with a sharp craft knife.

10 If any of the pencil line remains around the cut-out heart, gently rub it out.

11 Now lay your card open on your work surface with the cut-out to your left and the inside facing you.

12 Using the red and pink felt pens in rotation, write 'I LOVE YOU' all over the right-hand side of the card, making sure that each line starts with a different part of the message to avoid the words forming columns. Draw guidelines if you feel you need them.

13 When the ink is dry, close the card over a piece of scrap paper.

14 Using the red and pink felt pens alternately, and turning the card as necessary to be able to follow the shape of the heart, write 'I LOVE YOU' around the heart (see finished card).

15 Now do the same thing around the extreme outside edge of the card, starting in one corner and turning the card as you go. Try to finish at the end of a word at each corner .

16 Remove scrap paper and add your personal message – which, if you write one (for many valentines are anonymous!), will have to be written on the left-hand flap inside below the heart-shaped hole, or on the very back.

Variations

Instead of just two colours for the writing, try it with as many shades of pink as you can find. Some sets of coloured felt pens carry several different shades.

Try making this card out of pink card with gold writing. Perhaps place lace, or the outer part of a heart-shaped paper doily sprayed gold, around the heart as for the 'Pink Ribbon Valentine'.

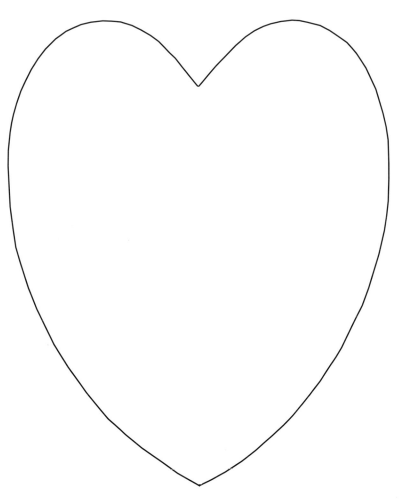

Full-size pattern for Project 12

Simple Painted Cards

Of all the techniques in this book, painting is the one which will make the most people apprehensive. So many individuals feel that they have no 'artistic talent' and that without it they will never be able to achieve anything pretty or successful. This is not the case. Anyone can produce pleasant effects with paint and enjoy doing so. The four cards in this section require nothing more than care and patience, and a determination to 'have a go'.

13 Simple Landscape

The design of this card is nothing more than a set of simple shapes filled in with colour and divided by lines of unpainted paper. The human brain constantly seeks to recognize and make sense of what it sees, and will 'see' a landscape in these shapes because of the colours. This is similar to looking for pictures in the fire, as we did as children. Try this project for the process of doing it as much as for the end result. Every child can tell you how pleasant it is to mix paint and do some colouring-in. There is really no more to it than that. Painted cards are good for every occasion – just add a message.

Materials

Card 1 x A4 photocopy card, pale green, light blue or white. When the painting is finished you will be able to decide which colour card looks best against it.

Water-Colour Paper You will need a reasonably smooth paper which is strong enough not to buckle too much when wet. I used a pad of cartridge drawing and painting paper. When painting, support the paper on its pad (even if you tear it off) or on a board.

Paper A5 sheet of photocopy paper.

Brush Soft water-colour brush.

Paint Acrylic in tubes or pots – you will need at least blue, red and yellow.

Palette You will need a plate, saucer or similar to mix paint on. You will rarely use the paint from the tub or pot, because it is quite thick – normally it will need to be diluted.

Book about 3cm thick, to prop up one end of your painting pad or board.

Board Use the sketch pad or a large, thin book to support the paper.

Masking Tape

Pencil and Rubber

Scrap Paper White, not newspaper.

Full-Sized Pattern for this card.

'L' Pieces These will create a frame for you while you decide how much of your painting to use.

Glue Pritt Stick or PVA.

Method

1 Place the A5 photocopy paper over the pattern for this picture, secure with small pieces of masking tape and trace.

2 Turn the tracing over and place it on scrap paper. Do not use newspaper for this, as the print might rub off onto your work.

3 With soft pencil, scribble over the back of the lines on the paper.

4 Now place the paper right side up onto the water-colour paper, which you should leave on the pad as it will keep the paper rigid. Keep the paper in place with small pieces of masking tape.

5 Go over the traced lines again, pressing quite hard. The scribbled pencil lead on

the back should leave a mark on the water-colour paper.

6 Discard the tracing.

7 If the lines on the water-colour paper are very faint, go over them with the pencil. These lines will be rubbed out later, so do not make them too dark. You just need to be able to see them.

8 Fix the water-colour paper to your chosen board with masking tape and prop against the book so the top of the picture is higher than the bottom. This will help the paint to flow down the paper.

9 Before you start to paint it is important to remember that you are going to leave the area on either side of the pencil lines white. Look at the finished picture – the white areas are where the lines were.

10 Mix up a watery puddle of mid-blue paint and, with the brush, paint a test

strip onto a scrap piece of white paper. You should be able to see the white of the paper shining through. If the paint obscures the paper it is too thick – add more water. Paint will dry lighter, but if it is too pale it can be painted over when dry, whereas if it is too dark there is little that can be done.

11 Take up plenty of paint in your brush. You are now going to put a wash of thin paint over the top (sky) area of your picture. Paint from the top down in horizontal strips from left to right. The slope will help the paint run down and cover more evenly. Remember to stop short of the pencil line.

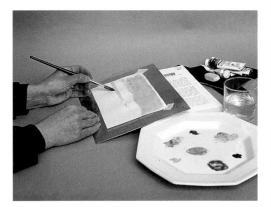

12 You may find that quite a lot of paint runs down and gathers at the bottom of the area you are painting. In this case, dry your brush on tissues and run it along the bottom where the paint is gathering. Because the brush is dry it will suck in the excess paint.

13 Now, using the same blue and working from top to bottom as usual, paint in section 2, which is the sea. Make sure you paint up to but not onto the cottage. This is the only place where you will paint right up to the pencil lines, so that its shape is clear (see finished card).

14 You have now painted all the blue areas, so touch the point of your brush into the yellow and mix it into the blue already on your palette. This should give you a green which you can use to paint sections 3, 4, 5 and 6. Add more yellow or blue, if you need to, to vary the green from area to area. Remember to remove any excess paint that gathers at the base of each section you paint. Continue to avoid all pencil lines except the cottage, which you must paint up to.

15 Now take a very small amount of red onto your brush and add to the green to produce a muddy brown. Use this to put a wash on section 7.

16 Remove any further build-up of paint at the bottoms of the sections with a dried brush as described above.

17 Leave all to dry, still propped up.

18 Take the dried painting and rub out the pencil lines, working the rubber along the lines and avoiding rubbing across the paint.

19 Put the painting onto a cutting surface and, using the 'L' pieces as described in Materials and Techniques, decide which part of the painting to trim off to make the best picture.

20 When you are satisfied, mark with a pencil where the inner sides of the 'L' pieces come to, and then cut along them.

21 Now take the A4 sheet of card and fold in half with short sides together.

22 Place the folded card on the work surface with the opening to the bottom.

23 Place your painting on the card centrally, and when you are happy with the position mark the card at the corners of the painting with a faint pencil mark.

24 Place your painting face down on scrap paper and spread glue all over the back, making sure that the edges are well glued.

25 Place the painting down on the card front.

26 Cover the card with scrap paper and weight with a heavy book until dry.

27 When the glue is dry, rub out the pencil marks and add a greeting to the inside, or leave blank as a letter card or notelet.

Variations

This technique of creating coloured sections divided by dry lines of unpainted card can be used to make a stained-glass window effect. Make a picture the same way, dividing it into sections, and colour in stronger, jewel colours. Then when all is dry fill in the white areas with black felt pen and mount on a black card.

You could try making your cards smaller.

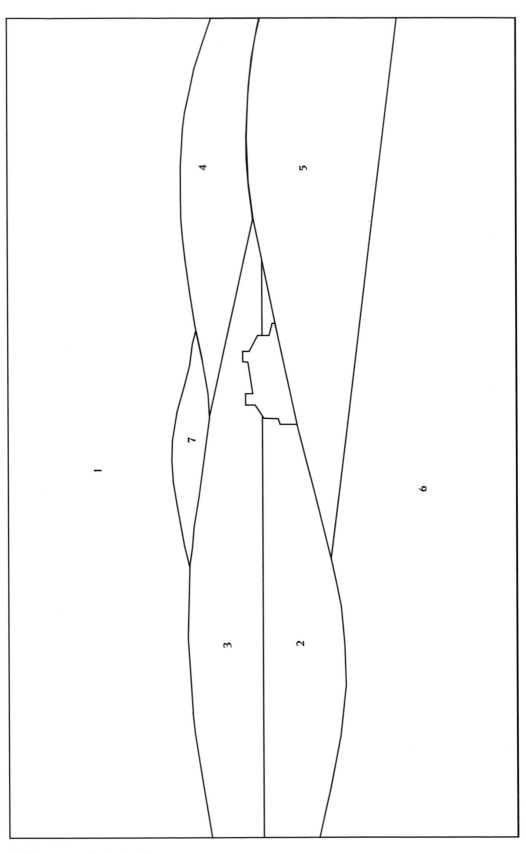

Full-size pattern for Project 13

14 Photocopy and Wash

Traditional 'pen and wash' pictures – original drawings in waterproof black ink with water-colour paint washed over in thin layers – are very pleasing, but what if you cannot do the initial ink drawing? In this project you can create a very similar picture by tracing a simple photograph and photocopying it to produce the black waterproof outlines to fill in with colour. You may find that your friends want to frame and display your cards, so keep messages to the inside!

Materials

Card 1 x A4 photocopy card, white.

Picture Photo, postcard or calendar picture of a simple scene, any size. If you cannot find a suitable scene then use my selected scene – the tracing is included. Instructions are given for my picture, but you can adapt them for a picture of your own choice.

Clear Plastic Sheet The sort used with overhead projectors, or a clear plastic folder.

Felt Pen Black, thin and permanent.

Photocopier

Masking Tape

Paint Acrylic in tubes or pots. You will need at least blue, red and yellow.

Palette An old plate or saucer will do to mix paint on.

Brush Water-colour paintbrush.

Scrap Paper Newspaper and white photocopier paper.

Board This can be any firm surface to support the card while it is being painted. A large cheese board or a large, thin book will do fine.

Book 3cm thick, to prop your board and card up on while painting.

Method

1 Place your selected picture on your work surface and secure it at the corners with masking tape. Secure the clear plastic sheet over it with more masking tape.

The Earl's Palace, Kirkwall, Orkney

2 Use the black permanent felt pen to trace the picture onto the plastic sheet. Some pens smudge, so use a piece of white scrap paper to cover the area you have already done if you have to put your arm or hand over it. To make a winter scene, put in tree branches but not leaves. If the leaves in the photo obscure the branches, sketch in a few branches where you think they should be. You cannot put in every detail of a picture but make sure that all the main outlines and features, like windows, are in.

3 Photocopy the design onto card. If you

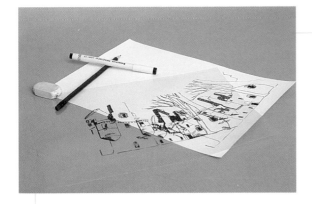

are not using my picture, which is already A5, get it blown up or reduced to A5 size and copied onto your A4 card. The orientation of the original will dictate which way round the picture will best fit on your card (see sketch).

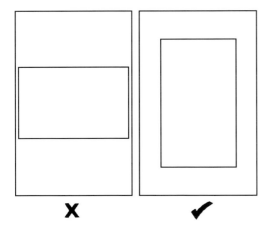

X   **✔**

4 Fold the card in half with short sides together.

5 Lay the card on the board so that the picture is towards you and prop the top edge on the book. Fix with masking tape.

6 Remember as you paint the picture that this is a winter scene and all flat

surfaces will be white with snow. This includes the tops of walls and horizontal branches, so leave a small amount of white paper at the tops of some of these (see finished card).

7 You will now have to mix some paint. With your brush take some of the blue onto the palette and add enough water to make a puddle of colour.

8 Try out the colour on a piece of scrap white paper. The paint should be thin enough for the white paper to shine through. If the paint totally obscures the paper it is too thick – add more water.

9 Take plenty of paint on your brush.

10 Paint the sky horizontally from left to right, moving down all the time from the top to the bottom. The slope of the board will help the paint to flow down the picture.

11 You may find that quite a lot of paint runs down and gathers at the bottom of the area you are painting. In this case, dry your brush on tissues and run it along the bottom where the paint is gathering. Because the brush is dry, it will suck in the excess paint.

12 Next mix in a small amount of red and yellow to the blue to make an indeterminate brown, and paint in the walls.

13 When the walls have dried, paint over the walls which are in shadow in your

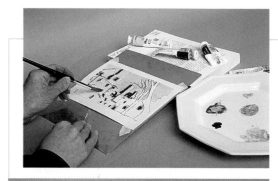

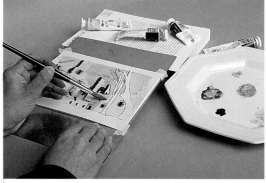

Variations

This card duplicates well and I once made 60, painting them 10 at a time – all the skies, then all the trees, etc.

This does not have to be a winter or Christmas picture – try the same card with grass and leaves. Try different landscapes or townscapes. Make smaller photocopies of your tracing and colour with coloured pencils for a lovely soft effect. Cut these out and mount them on smaller cards.

Try doing your painting on white water-colour paper and then cutting it to size and sticking it onto a card, as in the previous project. Use card that reflects the colours of the painting, rather than white.

photo with the same paint again, which will make them darker. Pick out window surrounds and odd stones in the lighter walls, or similar details in your own picture. This will add detail and interest.

14 Add more yellow or red to the brown to make a different shade, and paint the trunks and branches of the trees. Leave some patches of white to suggest snow. Let this dry (which will not take long) before proceeding, and then with the same paint run a shadow down the same side of each tree trunk (see finished card).

15 On a clean part of the palette put a small amount of blue and mix into it a little of the brown puddle of paint

to muddy the blue colour a little, then add some water. Use this to put in a few shadows on the snow and at the bases of the trees and walls (see finished card).

16 Leave the painting propped up and allow to dry completely.

17 With a ruler and a thick black felt pen, carefully draw a framing line around your picture.

18 Open the card and centrally on the inside write 'MERRY CHRISTMAS AND A HAPPY NEW YEAR'.

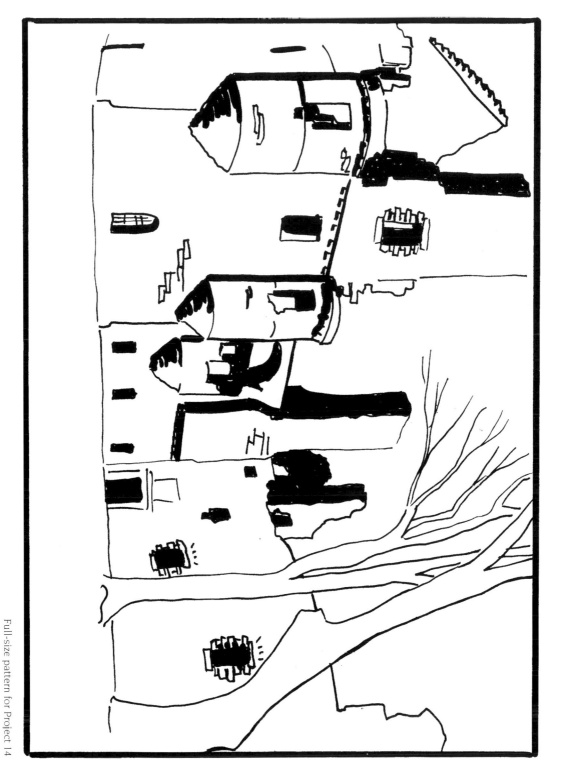

Full-size pattern for Project 14

15 Abstract Landscape

This project involves spreading and mixing various-coloured paints all over large sheets of white paper. Completely covering the paper is not necessary, as interesting effects can be found where colour and white meet. Then, by means of a simple cardboard frame, you select small parts which could suggest a landscape – sea and rocks, sunsets, etc. – and mount them on cards. Do not feel that you have to look only for landscapes – use any part that excites you. The section you decide to use can be any size, as quite small pieces can look wonderful once mounted.

Materials

Card I x A4 photocopy card, white.

Paper Several large sheets of cartridge paper.

Paint Acrylics or water-colours in tubes or pots but not pans. Any colours you have – the more the merrier, but at least three.

Scrapers Some squares of stiff card approximately 5–8cm square for scraping the paint around the surface of the paper.

'L' Pieces These two pieces of card will help you find the parts of the painting you want to keep; see Materials and Techniques for details of how to make them.

Masking Tape

Scissors Large ones to help you cut straight edges in one go.

Pencil and Rubber

Glue Pritt Stick or PVA.

Weight A large book, in a plastic bag for protection from paint and glue.

Scrap Paper Newspaper.

Method

1 Spread a piece of cartridge paper on your work surface and stick down with a bit of masking tape at each corner.

2 If you are using tubes of colour, squeeze out blobs of each colour of the paint you have down one side of the paper quite close together.

3 If you are using pots of colour, use a paint brush, teaspoon or strip of stiff card to transfer blobs of paint to your paper.

4 With one of the squares of stiff card, start to drag the colour around the paper. Spread all the paint to encourage interesting mixing.

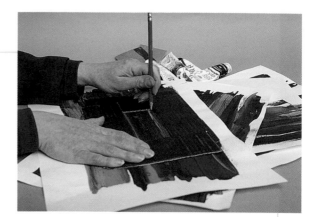

5 At this stage you may find that the paint is too thick. If so, try again on the next piece of paper with a little water trickled amongst the blobs prior to dragging. **Or**, if you do not seem to have much to drag, make the next blobs bigger. **Or**, make more blobs and dot around the paper. What you are aiming at is a piece of paper covered in colour, with swirling areas and mixing areas. Let yourself go.

6 Do as many sheets of paper as you want – you will find that they improve as you get the hang of it. Then let the papers dry.

7 Take your 'L' pieces and hold them together so that they form a rectangular window, the size of which is not important at present. You are going to look for interesting areas on the paintings. These may or may not suggest landscapes or sunsets – they may just be attractive mixtures of colour. Wherever you see something you like, select it. Even if you feel that the large sheets of paper are not at all interesting, the frames may make all the difference. Areas that are part colour and part white (unpainted) can be very attractive.

8 Move the window formed by the frames over the painted sheets of paper. When you come to an interesting bit, stop and move the two

parts of the frame to make the area you are interested in larger or smaller. Does this improve it or not?

9 Lay your frame down on the part you have decided to use and carefully draw around the inside of the frame with a pencil.

10 When you have found one or more attractive sections (depending on how many cards you want to make), cut these out. Repeat the following stages for each piece you have chosen.

11 Take your A4 sheet of card and fold in half with the short sides together.

12 Lay the card on the work surface with the opening to the bottom or to the right, depending on the shape of the painting.

13 Lay your chosen painting on the front of the card and position it centrally.

14 With a soft pencil, mark where the four corners are on the card.

15 Remove the painting and glue the area defined by the pencil marks. Try to avoid gluing the pencil marks, as glue will fix them and make it impossible to rub them out.

16 Stick the picture down on the glue and cover with some scrap paper. Put under a weight until dry.

17 Rub out the pencil marks.

18 Add a message to the front, perhaps 'Happy Birthday', or leave blank and use as a letter card or notelet.

Variations

This is a civilized version of children's finger-painting. If you do not mind getting very dirty, put your blobs of paint directly onto a washable kitchen work surface and spread and smear with your bare hands. Then, while the paint is still wet, press sheets of white paper down onto the paint and smooth them so that they are well coated. This is a sort of printing and produces surprising results.

Use fabric paints instead of ordinary paint and press white or coloured cotton down onto it, then fix as per the instructions and you have your own uniquely patterned fabric to use for small projects. Clean the work surface with a mildly abrasive cream.

Try making smaller cards so that you can utilize attractive scraps of painting, no matter how small. You should experiment to see what you personally like.

You could mount the painting on a rectangle of white card slightly bigger than it, and then mount the whole thing on a dark-coloured card chosen to match the predominant paint colour.

16 Sponging through a Window Template

By applying paint with a sponge over a template onto the card, you are creating the illusion of a window frame with something beyond. The blue above and green below suggest that that something is a garden – a suggestion you then strengthen by adding small dots of strong flower colours.

Materials

Card 1 x A4 sheet of photocopier card, white.

Paint Any paint will do for this as long as it is not runny. I have used acrylic, but you could try water-colour in tubes, or emulsion. You will need a mid blue, a dark and a light green, yellow and red.

Palette An old plate is fine.

Sponge A small natural sponge or a torn piece from a synthetic domestic one. You want something not too big, about the size of a small tomato.

Template B One in photocopier card and one in photocopier paper.

Pencil, Rubber and Ruler

Craft Knife (or Small Scissors) In this instance the knife will be easier to use.

Cutting Board

Masking Tape

Scrap Paper Newspaper.

Full-Size Window Pattern

Method

1 Tape the photocopier paper over the window pattern and trace carefully.

2 Carefully peel off the tracing plus tape from the table and pattern. Stick the tracing over the template made of card on a cutting surface.

3 Using a ruler to keep accurately to the lines, cut through the tracing and the card with the knife. Discard the tracing.

4 Fold the A4 sheet of card in half, short sides together.

5 Lay the folded card on the work surface with the opening to the right.

6 Tape the cut-out window over the front of the card. Make sure that the tape also secures the whole assembly to the work surface.

7 Wet the small sponge and squeeze out really well so that it is just damp.

8 Pat it on the scrap paper to make sure that it is not leaving wet marks.

9 Squeeze or spoon out some blue paint onto your palette and pat the sponge into it. Pat the sponge on the scrap paper to spread the paint over the sponge and to take some of the excess off.

10 Starting at the top of the template, pat with an up and down movement (do not wipe) down the window, gradually filling the top two-thirds of the upper holes. You should ideally have more paint, and therefore darker blue, to the top, fading to very pale (less paint) at the bottom of this area.

11 The sponge should now be almost bare of usable paint and can be used for the next colour without spreading blue into it. Do not wash the residual paint out as this will make the sponge too wet again.

12 Squeeze or spoon some dark green onto the palette, or add some yellow to the blue, and repeat the process above. This time work the paint up from the bottom so that there is almost no paint where the colours come together.

13 Pat the sponge on the scrap paper to take as much dark green off as possible.

14 Squeeze or spoon some light green onto the palette, or mix more yellow into the green that is left. Pat the sponge into the second green paint to get a light covering on it.

15 Pat on scrap paper lightly, then gently pat over the area of the picture which is already green. You are trying to achieve a surface which is two-tone – dark green overspotted with light green – rather like trees or bushes where some leaves will be catching the sun.

16 Let the paint dry. This should not take long as you have put it on very dry.

17 Squeeze or spoon some red paint onto the palette and spread into a film with a piece of card.

18 Dab sponge on the film of paint gently so that the raised areas only get lightly covered with red paint.

19 Dab the red paint over the green area to put a few red flowers into your garden.

Variations

Sponge through any simply shaped template (square, triangle) with a mixture of colours blended together. This will give a pleasant abstract effect. Or use a decorating stencil to create a single motif on a card (i.e. simple shapes like houses, ducks and fish).

This card lends itself to being made in quantity.

20 Repeat what you did with the red (steps 17–19), this time using yellow paint.

21 Remove the window template and leave to dry.

22 Write a message or greeting inside, or leave blank as a notelet.

Full-size pattern for Project 16

Printing Techniques

Since prehistory, when men made hand-prints on cave walls with red clay, people have decorated their environment and clothes by printing. Part of the charm of any such project is the irregularity inherent in printing. Do not expect every motif to come out perfectly every time. A range of printing possibilities is explored in this section. All the cards in this section lend themselves to being duplicated.

17 Potato Print
18 String Block Repeat
19 Printing with Found Objects
20 Rubber Stamp and Embossing
   Powder

17 Potato Print

Potatoes are freely available and easy to cut to shape, and so have been used for a long time to make simple but effective prints both on textiles and on paper.
The only drawback with using potatoes is that they do not last – they shrivel very quickly and so must be used the day they are made.
This card is made using four different flower shapes cut out of potato to make a fresh-looking Easter card.

Materials

Card 1 x A4 sheet photocopier card, green.

Potatoes You will need two potatoes, each cut in half. The cut surfaces of the halves have to be big enough to cut the flower designs from.

Knife A small vegetable knife with a point will be best.

Paint Any thick paint will do. I have used emulsion paint which comes in small trial-size pots, but acrylic will do fine. You will need four pastel shades – I have used pink, yellow, lilac and blue, again all readily available in test pots.

Paint Tray and Pad These will be needed unless you are using the sort of test-sized pots of emulsion which come with a brush in the lid.

Newspaper For testing, drying potatoes and protecting surfaces.

Paper 1 sheet of white photocopy paper.

Pencil

Scissors Small.

Felt Pen Gold or silver, and black for drawing on the potatoes.

Full-Sized Flower Patterns

Method

1 Place the white paper over each of the four flower designs and trace with the pencil.

2 Cut out all the flowers, and cut out their centres.

3 Cut each potato in half across its narrower measurement and place cut side down on the newspaper to dry the cut surface.

4 Place the first flower pattern on the cut surface of a potato half and draw round it with the black felt pen, which should write well enough on the dried surface.

5 Cut round the flower, removing excess to a depth of at least 1cm. Remove the centre as well, again to a good depth.

6 Draw and cut out the other three flowers in the same way.

7 Dry the faces of the cut potatoes again to make sure that there is no ink coming from the lines you drew.

8 Assign a colour of paint to each flower.

9 Taking any flower and its paint, dip your brush into the paint and paint the flower surface only of the stamp.

10 On newspaper, test that the stamp makes a reasonable print – some irregularities will enhance the design, but you want the shape to be clear. Experiment to see how many prints you can get from the potato before it needs to be repainted.

11 Fold the A4 sheet of card in half with short sides together.

12 Lay the folded card on the work surface with the opening to the right.

13 Insert a large sheet of scrap paper inside the card to protect the back from paint.

14 You are going to cover the right-hand side and lower part of the card front in flower stamps, some overlapping, leaving a triangle of green card in the top left-hand area for the greeting (see finished card).

15 Repaint your first stamp and print a flower gently near the bottom left of the card.

16 Without repainting (if possible), print another flower to the right and higher than the first. The differences in intensity of the prints, because they are not all newly painted, will add to the design.

17 Print two or three flowers with each of the other stamps, allowing some flowers to overlap slightly and some to overlap the edge of the card. Repaint the stamps as necessary.

18 Continue in this way until you are happy with the design. Refer to the picture of the finished card for help.

19 Allow to dry completely.

20 Using the gold or silver felt pen, write 'HAPPY EASTER' in the unpainted area of the front, referring to the finished card for positioning. Draw pencil guidelines if necessary.

21 Put an Easter or personal message inside.

Variations

Rather than use a metallic pen, use a felt pen which tones with one of the flower colours. These floral stamps can be used for any number of objects – cards, wrapping paper and letter headings. Remember to make everything you want with these stamps the day you make them, as they will shrivel very quickly.

Full-size patterns for Project 17

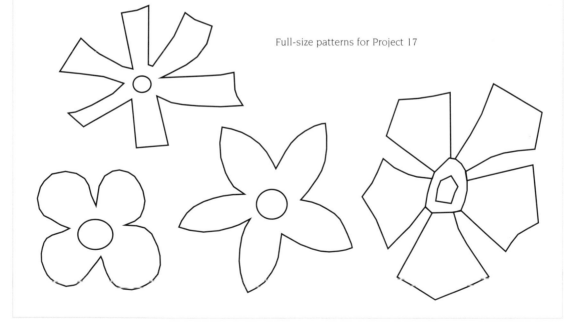

18 String Block Repeat

A limitless variety of finished prints is available from just a small block, some string and some paint. Once you have successfully created and used this print block you will be eager to try out other shapes, different colours and new layouts. See the suggested variations at the end of this project – I am sure you will be able to think of many more yourself.

Materials

Card I x A4 photocopier card, black.
String Thick cotton parcel string.
Printing Block 1cm or more thick. This could be a piece of wood or thick polystyrene packaging. I have used the latter.
Craft Knife, if using polystyrene.
Wood Saw, if using wood block.
Glue PVA or Copydex are definitely best for this project.
Brushes You will need a brush for the glue and a small brush for the gold paint.
Paint Gold – a small tin of the sort of enamel or acrylic paint sold for model-makers. Consult the tin for how to clean the brush.
Gold Marker Pen
Scrap Paper
Scissors Large.
Black Felt Pen, Pencil and Rubber
Template B in copy paper.

Method

1 Fold template B in half and then in half again.

2 Open out the paper and fold in half in the other direction, then in half again.

3 You now have the paper divided into 16 equal rectangles.

4 Cut out one rectangle – the large scissors will help keep the sides straight. This is your pattern for the printing block.

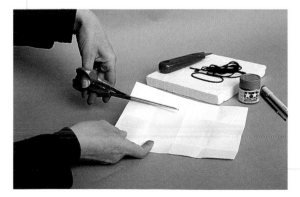

5 Mark round the pattern onto the polystyrene with the black pen, or onto the wood with the pencil, and cut out.

6 With the pen or pencil draw a zigzag design on the surface of the block. The curved line should not be too close together and the turns or corners should be rounded rather than sharp. Keep it simple.

7 Spread PVA or Copydex over the whole face of the block and stick the string down to follow the line you drew. Start at one end with the end of the string and cut off the excess when you reach the other end.

there is too much paint it will smudge – a second print without repainting may be much better. If so, while making the card, make the first print on scrap paper each time the string is repainted.

8 Make sure that the ends are securely glued.

9 Allow to dry.

10 If using PVA, brush another layer of glue over the whole face of the block and the string. This will seal the string onto the block.

11 Take the A4 card and fold it in half with the short sides together.

12 Lay the card on your work surface with the opening to the right and close a large sheet of scrap paper inside it to protect the back while you are printing.

13 Paint some gold paint onto the string and do a test print on scrap paper. If

14 Too little paint will not make a clear impression, so repaint and try again.

15 When you are happy with the result, start to print in the top left-hand corner. As both the card and the block are rectangular, make sure that they are both the same way round. The short side of the block should be to the short side of the card.

16 Print four repeats across the top of the card and then three down the right side (the first of the side prints is already there). Next print three along the bottom and the remaining two up the left side. Refer to finished card if unsure.

17 Allow to dry.

18 With the gold felt pen write 'An Invitation' or your own greeting in the middle of the front of the card, with each word below the last.

19 Write your personal message inside the card – also in gold, as an ordinary pen will not show up on the black card.

20 Try printing these blocks around the edge of the envelope as well for a co-ordinated look.

Variations

Instead of just framing the card in prints, fill in the whole front of the card (16 repeats). Use as a letter card.

Make small cards with single prints on them, or print both the card and envelope down the left-hand side only. Make the envelope from black paper so that they look like a set.

19 Printing with Found Objects

A 'found' object is anything which can be covered in paint and used to print onto a card. Round shapes can be produced with the ends of pencils or dowel, circles can be printed with the ends of kitchen-roll tubes. There are many objects made in the shape of something else, like biscuit-cutters, erasers and bath sponges, all of which can be found shaped like animals and fish, rockets and men. By looking around your own home you should be able to find some of these to be used in future projects. However, I have looked to nature for my found objects. Nothing makes a print which looks like a leaf as well as a real leaf does. I have provided a contrast to all the green by printing a few small leaves in gold.

Materials

Card 1 x A4 photocopier card, green or white.

Leaves Pick several small fresh leaves from trees and bushes and use them right away, or they will wilt and be useless. The best leaves are those that have raised veins on their backs.

Paint Several shades of green. Acrylic mixed with water to the consistency of cream or emulsion paint will be suitable. A small pot of acrylic or enamel gold paint and a small brush –

make sure you check the brush-cleaning instructions.

Paint Tray and Pad For the green paints. Any shallow container will do, even a dinner plate. Make the pad by cutting a kitchen sponge cloth to fit flat in the bottom of the tray.

Scrap Paper White photocopier paper for test prints and 3–4 sheets of newspaper for a pad to press down the leaves when printing.

Method

1 Fold the card in half with the short sides together.

2 Place the card on your work surface with the opening to the right.

3 Pour enough paint into the tray to saturate the pad but not have a layer of paint above it. Laying the pad into the paint and then carefully turning it over to wet the other side saturates it quickly.

4 Press the front of a spare leaf onto the pad, making sure that every part of the leaf is in contact with the paint.

5 Place the leaf carefully paint side down on scrap paper and, laying a

pad of scrap paper on top, smooth over the whole area with the flat of your hand, pressing lightly and evenly. (**NOTE** For the sake of clear photographs I have not used this pad, but it helps even printing.)

6 Take off the scrap paper and leaf and you should have a reasonable print of the leaf's veins. It does not have to be perfect, as irregularities add to the charm, but it should be recognizable. If it is only a blob of paint, then the paint may be too thin and deep, or you may have exerted too much pressure when printing. Try again, each time with a fresh leaf, as they soon spoil.

7 When you are happy with the result, take a fresh leaf and print it onto the card.

8 Print each time with new paint, and with different leaves, overlapping the prints and adding different shades of green to the pad as necessary until you are happy with the result. A very few prints or a clutter of different images can both be attractive.

9 With the brush, paint a very small leaf with gold paint. Print gold leaves into any spaces that may exist amongst the larger green leaves.

10 Allow to dry.

11 Open the card out and print a single small gold leaf on the middle top of the right-hand flap inside the card.

12 Use as a notelet or add a message of your choice.

Variations

Print the leaves in an unexpected colour like red, purple and pink on different-coloured card. Print up an envelope to match the card.

20 Rubber Stamp and Embossing Powder

For this project you will have to buy various things: a rubber stamp, an ink pad and some embossing powder. These are increasingly available in many shops, but if you experience any trouble then try any good craft or art shop, or buy direct from a rubber-stamp maker – try the *Yellow Pages*. This initially large outlay can be offset by the number of times the stamp and its pad can be used. For this reason I have selected an attractive stamp with no particular significance. Obviously you will get far less use out of a valentine or Easter motif. Finding and choosing the stamp is the hard part of this project, after which all will be pleasure.

Materials

Card 1 x A4 sheet of photocopier card, black.

Bought Rubber Stamp A wide range is available. Buy what you like. If it is bigger than mine do fewer repeats, if smaller make more repeats.

Ink Pad Buy this at the same place as the stamp.

Embossing Powder Again, buy this at the same place as the stamp.

Scrap Paper Two sheets of white photocopier paper.

Scissors Large or small.

Felt Pen Gold.

Pencil and Ruler

WARNING As this process requires the use of quite a lot of heat, a child should get an adult to heat the embossing powder, or simply do the prints without going on to do the embossing.

Method

1 Take the rubber stamp and its ink pad and stamp a few practice prints onto the scrap paper.

2 Allow the prints to dry – this will be a very short time.

3 Cut out each print.

4 Fold the card in half with the short sides together.

5 Place the card on the work surface with the open side to the right.

6 Position the cut-out prints on the front of the card in a pleasing arrangement – which may not be the same as mine, because the stamps will not necessarily be the same size.

7 When you are happy with the arrangement, mark the position of each print, very lightly, with the pencil.

8 Now print directly onto the card in those positions and, for each motif, while the ink is still wet, scatter embossing powder over the ink. The powder will soak into the ink and then you can knock off the excess. Save it

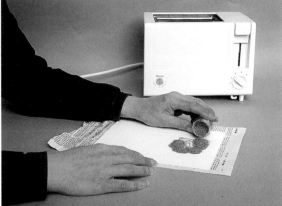

kept moving all the time to avoid scorching.

10 Allow to cool and add your personal message inside.

11 With the ruler and gold felt pen draw a line all around the outside edge of the front of the card.

by tapping the card on its edge over a scrap sheet of paper and pouring the powder back into its container. Do this for each motif in turn.

9 Now you must apply heat to the embossed area. This can be done using a heat gun (used for do-it-yourself jobs such as paint-stripping), the ring on an electric cooker, or a toaster. If the embossing powder is not hot enough it will not work, but overheat the card and it may discolour or even singe. I am afraid it is necessary to experiment. I have used the heat from a switched-on electric toaster. The card must be

Variations

There are so many rubber stamps available that the variations are endless. Ring the changes with different-coloured inks and embossing powders. On a narrow piece of similar card, stamp the same design, cut out and add a small tassel at the bottom to make a bookmark. Enclose the bookmark in the card as a small gift to go with the best wishes.

Conclusion: Where do we Go from Here?

Having reached this far in the book, you have probably already made some if not all of the projects featured. I hope that you have enjoyed the creative process and have a selection of cards of which you can be proud. Whilst you were following the instructions and making your cards you may have had ideas to simplify, modify or entirely change the method of working or the finished design. Why not have a go now at trying out some of those ideas – be your own designer!

If you do not feel inspired at present, why not try out some of the suggestions for variations which I have listed at the end of each project? These include making cards larger or smaller, changing their colours or their purpose, and making envelopes to match. There are many different ways to alter the basic ideas, particularly in the sections on painting and printing.

Try considering which of the cards lend themselves to being made in large numbers. Photocopied or printed cards will be very easy to prepare in bulk. Christmas cards in particular are bought and sold in their thousands every year, so perhaps you can find a simple way to make all you will need for next Christmas. Unspecified blank cards and birthday cards are handy to have a stock of in case you need one in a hurry.

All the cards in this book would benefit from having matching envelopes. As you know, the cards have been made to fit existing envelopes of C5 size, but why not customize these envelopes by writing, printing or painting some part of the design from their cards onto them? Remember to use waterproof materials!

Refer to the chapter on Making your own Envelopes. Try an envelope made from Christmas wrapping paper for Christmas cards, birthday wrapping paper for birthday cards, coloured paper to match the card, etc. The extra effort will be well worth it and give eye-catching results.

You should be in a position by now never to have to buy another card unless you really want to, and you may find that when friends receive your handmade cards they will want to know how they can get something similar for themselves. This could be your opportunity to design and make cards especially for them.

To take the idea of making cards for others further, you could look for another, more commercial outlet for your hobby. Perhaps there are craft fairs in your area where you would be made very welcome and advised on how to sell what you make. Local shops might also sell some cards for you. If you make cards for resale it is worth sticking to what you enjoy doing and finding ways to make several at a time without losing quality. Remember to cost out your materials and your time and add a small profit margin. Be realistic – the shop also has to add a profit margin.

What else can you do with your new-found skills? Why not look beyond cards and see what else you could make? Try producing decorative letterheads with made or bought stamps. Using the Writing, Painting and Printing techniques, create your own wrapping paper for any occasion. This could be made to match your cards. Gift cards which are also made to match would be an attractive addition. As well as making wrapping paper, write with fabric pens, or paint and print with fabric paint, to make a fabric design which can be made permanent by ironing. Use your unique material to make scarves, tablecloths and napkins. All the methods which produced landscape or abstract pictures for your cards can be made larger if desired, mounted and framed. These will look charming hanging on your walls.

Adapt some of the ideas in this book for home decorating. Something as simple as a potato can be made into a star stamp to print a nursery ceiling. The possibilities are only limited by your imagination – have a go and, most importantly, enjoy it!

About the Author

Pat Sutherland was born in Malta of an RAF family. She was educated in Scotland and England, doing a Diploma in Education at Aberdeen College of Education. After marrying Bruce in 1973 she worked in London for a few years, before moving to Orkney. She became a full-time housewife when her sons were born: Craig, who is now 19 and pursuing a career in golf, and Ian, now 14 and still at school. She took secretarial studies while her children were small, and currently works as an administration manager.

Over the last few years she has been an undergraduate with the Open University, where she has just received her BA.

Pat has always been interested in art and crafts, and is a member of her local Craftsmen's Guild.

TITLES AVAILABLE FROM
GMC Publications

BOOKS

WOODWORKING

WOODTURNING

Tatting Collage . . . . .Lindsay Rogers
Temari: A Traditional Japanese Embroidery Technique . . . . .Margaret Ludlow

THE HOME

Home Ownership: Buying and Maintaining . . . . .Nicholas Snelling
Security for the Householder: Fitting Locks and Other Devices . . . . .E. Phillips

---

VIDEOS

Drop-in and Pinstuffed Seats . . . . .David James
Stuffover Upholstery . . . . .David James
Elliptical Turning . . . . .David Springett
Woodturning Wizardry . . . . .David Springett
Turning Between Centres: The Basics . . . . .Dennis White
Turning Bowls . . . . .Dennis White
Boxes, Goblets and Screw Threads . . . . .Dennis White
Novelties and Projects . . . . .Dennis White
Classic Profiles . . . . .Dennis White
Twists and Advanced Turning . . . . .Dennis White
Sharpening the Professional Way . . . . .Jim Kingshott
Sharpening Turning & Carving Tools . . . . .Jim Kingshott
Bowl Turning . . . . .John Jordan
Hollow Turning . . . . .John Jordan
Woodturning: A Foundation Course . . . . .Keith Rowley
Carving a Figure: The Female Form . . . . .Ray Gonzalez
The Router: A Beginner's Guide . . . . .Alan Goodsell
The Scroll Saw: A Beginner's Guide . . . . .John Burke

MAGAZINES

**Woodturning • Woodcarving • Furniture & Cabinetmaking
BusinessMatters • Creative Ideas for the Home • The Router**

The above represents a full list of all titles currently published or scheduled to be published. All are available direct from the Publishers or through bookshops, newsagents and specialist retailers. To place an order, or to obtain a complete catalogue, contact:

GMC Publications,
166 High Street, Lewes, East Sussex BN7 1XU, United Kingdom
Tel: 01273 488005 Fax: 01273 478606

Orders by credit card are accepted

GMC Publications